Gaunisala Ni Bula

Keith Gregory

Published in Australia by Sid Harta Publishers Pty Ltd,
ABN: 46 119 415 842
23 Stirling Crescent, Glen Waverley, Victoria 3150 Australia
Telephone: +61 3 9560 9920, Facsimile: +61 3 9545 1742
E-mail: author@sidharta.com.au

First published in Australia 2018
This edition published 2018
Copyright © Keith Gregory 2018
Cover design, typesetting: WorkingType (www.workingtype.com.au)

The right of Keith Gregory to be identified as the Author of the Work has been asserted in accordance with the Copyright, Designs and Patents Act 1988.

The Author of this book accepts all responsibility for the contents and absolves any other person or persons involved in its production from any responsibility or liability where the contents are concerned.

All rights reserved. No part of this publication may be reproduced, stored in a retrieval system, or transmitted, in any form or by any means without the prior written permission of the publisher, nor be otherwise circulated in any form of binding or cover other than that in which it is published and without a similar condition being imposed on the subsequent purchaser.

Gregory, Keith
Gaunisala Ni Bula
ISBN: 978-1-925230-49-9
pp170

Me in Taveuni, Fiji wearing a bula shirt and office sulu. This is what I usually wear in Fiji.

Foreword

Gaunisala Ni Bula; the name is in Fijian. It means "Road of Life." Why did I select this title? A real and very cold "road of life" inspired the title. This was the ice road that went across Lake Ladoga, Europe's largest lake. When the Germans besieged Leningrad in World War 2 between 1941 and 1943 they had locked the city in an icy embrace that was one of the worst sieges in terms of lives lost in history. Trucks had to travel across the frozen lake to supply Leningrad while the Germans made life extremely difficult with bombing, shelling and strafing the convoys.

It reflects what has been my road of life in many ways. My life has been one where I have likewise had to endure some very testing times and often it has felt like there is only a narrow road that is keeping me sane and alive. The fact that I am both is an absolute miracle with many witnesses — Christian and non-Christian — who can testify to that fact.

This book is not only a story of my rather miraculous survival against some trying odds but also a testament of my own Christian beliefs, which feature prominently. My purpose is not to preach; rather, it has to clearly demonstrate what the case was.

There is an old conversation that begins when a man who has a lousy boss asks God, 'Why are things the way they are?' God tells him, 'Well, you know what it is like to be treated roughly, so now you know how not to treat other people.' As you read this book, the purpose of its title becomes very relevant indeed.

Dedication

To, A. Those many friends who showed me His ways and helped me. Whether you speak Warlpiri Yolngu, Arrernte Kukiyau Kriol, Tok Pisin, Indonesian, Italian, Fijian, or Aussie, English or Russian; this one is for you. Thanks.

Contents

Chapter		Page
1	How to Build a Skyscraper	3
2	Setting the stage	9
3	Living with Big Daddy; Bougainville 1975	15
4	St Barnabas School Ravenshoe; A short time lasts a lifetime	23
5	Reasons to reject Christianity based on St Barnabas experiences, and why they are flawed	33
6	Alice Springs and a rough start to adulthood!	43
7	Is there life after Alice Springs?	51
8	Asking the impossible, 'Are you ready?'	57
9	Restart in Darwin	63
10	Accident number two	75
11	Ni Sa Bula Nia Viti... (Welcome to Fiji)	85
12	When things go pear shaped; Fiji 1999-2000	91
13	Healing Time; Sydney 2000	99
14	Judging and understanding; new friends in Sydney	107
15	When they build the Railway	111
16	Winning your impossible war; how to prevail.	121
17	Elliott: A town that cries out	125
18	How not to operate in another culture	133
19	The 50-metre-long ravens	141
	Conclusion	151

Part 1

Chapter 1

How to Build a Skyscraper

Why have I called the first chapter what I have? It started with a walk in Sydney City in 2000. I was passing a huge hole in the ground with a crane in it, the tip of the lifting arm or jib was about my eye level which meant the hole was about twenty-five metres deep and there was concrete already poured under the crane! I felt that this was a great example of how a restoration of one's life should be. The work you never see is the foundation when the building is finished. There is little to betray the fact that a good twenty-five metres or more of it is the foundation. However, if you do not get the invisible part of it right, your building will not grace the skyline of your city for long.

Writing an often-hard book about hard times and the way one has managed to rise above them is like building that skyscraper. The work begins long before the pen goes to paper. This book began life in 1999 in Fiji as my marriage was starting to unravel. The idea was abandoned and not revisited before 2017. At the time, I was not ready to write something like it. But why?

Again, the construction of our hypothetical skyscraper comes into play; the environment that the book covers ranges from blessings to triumphs, but it also plumbs the depths of mental and physical abuse and other forms of mistreatment. It involves alcoholism, divorce, and other problems and happenings that hurt others and myself terribly. For instance, I have been married three times, each marriage ending in big financial loss and emotional injury. Therefore, the first thing is to write from a position of forgiveness that is firmly rooted in the Christianity I profess to serve and the Lord who is the head of it. It involves expressing that forgiveness by protecting, as much as possible, those who hurt me as well as those who have been hurt. They both need the protection of a book written with wisdom.

A major section of the foundation of my hypothetical skyscraper is forgiveness and a spirit of reconciliation and understanding; understanding where the person who did wrong was actually coming from. As a Christian, I firmly believe this understanding starts by praying for your enemies and those who hate you. Is this not mentioned in the Bible I profess to follow? Once you understand this, a flow of ideas begins and a strategy begins to form as to how to positively deal with them. You begin to see what motivated them to dislike you. Sometimes it is what you have done. Other times it is that they are just that way by nature. Then the "Why?" comes into play. This means that a flow starts; understanding reinforces forgiveness, which makes you pray for that person. This has often undermined the hate or bitterness against that person as their own story becomes clearer. It is a fact that in most cases, they have apologised or I have done so, and in many cases, we became close friends.

The question arises as to whether or not one can forgive those who did the wrong thing and simply mention the matter as a fact of history, without injuring the person who did it. After all, that person has since got on with life, and in most cases became a decent person. Therefore, how to do things in a forgiving manner is a major skill in this situation.

For example, a situation may arise that affects your life deeply. It may be that you have been seriously abused at a boarding school and absolutely none of your family believes you — and they never will, either. How do you live with that? Forgive them and get on with it? A prayer I learned at an AA meeting has served me well and acted as a centre to build my other plans around: "Lord, help me accept the things I cannot change, the courage to change the things I can, and the wisdom to know the difference." This is a prayer that I've had to make an integral part of my life. You will never get them to apologise for what they did and justice may be a waste of time to pursue. Therefore, the only option open to you to limit the damage and save your own sanity and happiness is to obey what you believe as a Christian and forgive, which is a hard task. The fact that it is hard kept the writing of this book in limbo for nineteen years.

Therefore, as I write, I have decided to change or omit all together the names of persons who did whatever they did. I have simply mentioned the deed as fact. To do otherwise is a clear breach of my own beliefs that I uphold. It also expresses a wish to see them not be damaged by what I write here, but also they must see that this book is written in a way that does not scatter them, but attracts them to His grace and forgiveness and restoration.

As we progress with the foundations of the hypothetical skyscraper, we come to the next part of the foundation: taking personal responsibility. Regardless of the circumstances, I make it quite plain that I insist on taking responsibility for my actions and decisions, ones that were influenced by circumstances that acted to propel me down the road I took. That I could not stop drinking, fighting or sleeping around is one thing. I had to make a firm decision to be humble enough to firstly admit I was way out of control, and the next was to trust the Lord Jesus that He would forgive me my many sins and help me sort it out as it was way beyond my own ability.

Finally, the road I have travelled has featured a working past with Eastern Europeans (Greeks, Russians), Italians, Chinese, Indonesians and a host of many other nationalities as well as refugees from many parts of the globe. It features my long relationship with Aboriginal and Islander people as well as those from West Papua, PNG, Bougainville and Fiji. The traditions that I learned out of this and the spiritual environment had a huge influence on my politics, my beliefs and the way I now view the world in general. Therefore, the exercise is to take what is good in those cultures and use them. The rule of thumb then becomes how to line what your reactions and your interactions are with those cultures with what one saw Jesus do in the way He walked. As a Christian, I must debate and react with alternative thoughts and lifestyles as Jesus would have done which is a major challenge in often emotive and politically charged debates. Often the stereotypical Christian does not deal with these areas in line with what the Lord they profess to serve would do. This fact is in many a paper and social network and has done no service to Christianity to the many readers of this book.

Therefore, if a Christian is whom they say they are, then the Bible does admonish them to respect others to preserve a good witness and to pray for those around them. In 1 Corinthians 6:12, Paul states that one has the right to do anything but not all things are beneficial. In addition, Galatians 5:13-14 says, "You, my brothers and sisters, were called to be free. But do not use your freedom to indulge the flesh; rather, serve one another humbly in love."

My life has been a story of many cultures; this book spans

Australia, PNG, Fiji, and NT and Qld in particular. In many of the cultures I've been exposed to, there are protocols to observe that are strict. In many ways, the knowledge that has been entrusted to you, you have to be very careful with. To be reckless with some of the information I know regarding cultural matters could have severe consequences for myself both physically and spiritually. To simply adopt a cavalier attitude towards such things, or follow a strictly secular view of them is a major reason why the papers and conversations of many feature government programmes are failing and why even some church missions fail.

For instance, there are many Australian Indigenous friends who have passed away and there is a rule in many of their cultures that their name must not be mentioned deliberately. If you do by any chance mention it in ignorance, then you say sorry and do not mention it again. Surname is OK but given name is not permitted to be mentioned in most Aboriginal traditional settings. Therefore, you will see the term Kumanjayi referring to a person throughout if it is an Indigenous person who has passed on. In addition, there is reference to other aspects of traditional aspects of Fijian, PNG, and Aboriginal culture.

This book is not only to show a person the way that my belief in Christ has shaped my life and saved me from an early grave many times. It is also an attempt to show people, by using my own experiences, how to apply the Scripture to what might be a situation where those who profess to uphold it behave in a way that is completely incompatible with it or with any common decency.

As we progress through, there are many instances where the church, especially the Pentecostal Church in general, have overstepped their biblical, legal and ethical boundaries.

However, it must be stressed that the vast majority of the church in general is not like that and the workers in them are often the highest people of integrity doing a very hard job. In fact, a pastor is in the top ten of professions that are subject to what's known as "burn out". Right up there with police, emergency workers and other such professions. Any objective and sensible examination of their roles in society must take the above into consideration.

Chapter 2

Setting the stage

What were the biggest influences on me? Firstly, as with anyone, it is one's family. My family is from the UK. My father was an electrician and Mum was a stay-at-home mum as far as I know. I was born in Luton, UK in 1966, the youngest of three. My parents migrated to Australia in 1969, and followed the work. We started our Australian lives in Melbourne at a migrant's quarters in Burwood. In 1970, we undertook a trek that in anybody's language was a daring feat for a new migrant family and three screaming kids. They drove across the Nullarbor when the road was still a goat track. I have actually retraced the original highway, and it would have been quite challenging in a Ford Falcon station wagon. We ended up at Wundowie, just east of Perth in Western Australia, 4000km west of Melbourne on the other side of Australia! Then Armadale, in front of the brick works on Albany Highway. After that, we went up to North West Cape, arriving there in 1972 and staying until 1974. Exmouth was an American base with a large VLF antenna (the largest then in the Southern Hemisphere). There was good fishing there, and a reasonably good lifestyle. That was where I started school. It was a town with everything American, even collisions, as the Americans drove down the wrong side of the road. The US houses were very well built and the Aussie ones were fibro-clad ones on stilts.

My father worked for the US Navy. We had a boat and would regularly go fishing in what was one of the best fishing spots in Australia and the clearest waters anywhere around.

I remember several things about Exmouth. Firstly, there was my rather shaky start to school; secondly, the time when my dad flipped the boat over with Ian, my eldest brother, and a friend on board just before we left; and thirdly, things were expensive in Exmouth so we used to go to Carnarvon, a bone-shaking 300km of dirt road away, if we wanted to do any major shopping. They sealed it just before we left. Finally, race relations in 1970's WA; the sign on a roadhouse door near Carnarvon was a tin sign, white with black lettering stating "NO BLACKS PERMITTED!" Again, the sign had a lasting impact on me. I was that disgusted with the place that I never bought anything there until recently. Little did I know that the Indigenous people it forbade entry to would be such a large and treasured part of my life as a teenager and as an adult.

The racism against Aboriginals was a feature of the state as were many attractions and beauty. There were very crude jokes about them. Being compared to them would often start fights at school. Added to that, Exmouth had no Aboriginals that I knew of. In fact, one of the church elders in a church I attended said, 'We didn't have an Aboriginal problem in Exmouth!' That was in 2002! Think back to the final pages of the last chapter. I dusted off my feet from that church because racism of that nature was simply beyond my comprehension.

In fact, the reason it only partially surfaced was that Mum and Dad would often hear of stories, usually bad ones, regarding them. They had not had any exposure to these people other than what they had heard from mates who themselves had heard stories second- or even third-hand.

In addition, there were the "Indigenous Fish Stories" as I call them now — the inflated stories of what they got from the government that grew even more outlandish as the story went around. Even as a young kid I found them unbelievable and when I went to Ravenshoe where I was at boarding school, I thought they were rubbish, even though I knew next to nothing about policy towards Aboriginal people other than that it was paternalist or downright racist. I am utterly amazed that many adults still believe these stories, and spread them about the place like garbage spread about by the wind.

This shaped the racial attitudes both my parents had. Another factor was the era and the environment they came from. This was an England being shorn of its empire; those who could were deserting the colonies, and their presence fanned a xenophobia that still features in any Western country's politics today. Dad was a workaholic who lived for his work, and thought the best way to look after his family was to work and raise the cash. Generally, I think that when he was on his own he was very open to anyone, and would often help anyone, but he definitely would not take any of their rubbish! In short, a man who lived for his work and had a very practical view of the world.

As far as God was concerned, I think Mum started out as a committed Christian and went to Exmouth as one, and Dad believed in God and professed to be a Christian. As for me, I had a basic belief in God and that was, well, all there was to it. However, a few issues surfaced in Exmouth that would shape the whole of my school years and our family.

I started in Grade One, and then problems arose that resulted in two trips to Perth to see an assessor. They recommended that I should be dropped back to pre-school, which is exactly what happened in term three. Then in 1973, I went up to Grade One again.

Exmouth was known for an extremely high divorce rate. It was also extremely isolated with shift-work often aggravating tensions in a marriage that might not be so potentially catastrophic to it in a less challenging environment.

In fact, when I returned to Exmouth in 2002, one thing the new owner of the place we lived in remarked on was that each owner, after we left, had one thing in common; they all separated or divorced, including themselves.

In 1974, we left Exmouth to go to Perth, to a place named Girrawheen, where we ended up in a Housing Commission flat on Golders Way. At that time, the suburb formed the eastern edge of the built-up area and was only a few years old at the time. Drew, my elder brother, and I went to the local primary school and Ian to the local high school. Dad found work there at a factory we called Fred Talk; its actual name was F.R. Talk. He was only there a short time because a job he wanted more was coming up. It was the job with the huge mine in Bougainville in PNG. In April he left, but we stayed an additional year in Perth.

I went from Grade Two to Grade Three, but there were considerable problems. The first was that the suburb was a new one, and the Housing Commission sent quite a lot of people on welfare, and with low paid jobs, there. It was fertile ground for mischief. Ian was the worst affected, being the eldest, and we other two were not so much, but slowly the influence of the environment, plus Dad's absence, made it difficult to keep out of bad company, which in our case was right up to the front door. Had we not gone to Bougainville, I think I would have descended into a highly corrosive environment and ended up in the Criminal Justice System long before I actually did.

Chapter 3

Living with Big Daddy; Bougainville 1975

The next stop was Bougainville Island; these days the mention of that name brings a laugh in Australia. This is because "Bogan" is actually a class of person these days in Australia. Well, imagine if you had to say you came from another island because your own island was unjustly made an object of ridicule by often unthinking people. You wouldn't like it, would you? Therefore, why do this to the intelligent and talented people of the island of Bougainville?

It was named after a French explorer, Luis de Bougainville, who bumped into it in 1790. First, it belonged to Britain, then Germany, then after 1914 it was Australian mandated territory. An interesting note here is that if you were born in Port Moresby prior to 1975 you had Australian Citizenship at birth. If you were born on Bougainville, you had no right to Australian citizenship as they were under different administrative structures. Of course, Bougainville was swapped between Britain and Germany and became just one more of those funny (or not so funny, if you are from West Papua) colonial mismatches with scant regard for who was "in" and who was "out", consisting of very different people from mainland PNG. Bougainville is one of the larger Pacific Islands, as well as one of the most unstable politically. The fact that it is the northernmost of the Solomon Islands and has little in common with the rest of PNG also feeds the politics of the island in a major way.

The copper mine was run by Bougainville Copper Limited, an Australian company that was a subsidiary of CRA (now Rio Tinto). We called Bougainville Copper "Big Daddy" because the expatriates were looked after very well by the mine and though the locals (or nationals) were much lower paid the same applied. In 1965, a geologist discovered more of what was already known to exist in the southern mountains of the island — a massive low-grade copper deposit with gold and silver credits. The mine was set up at a time when Australia was attempting to make PNG independent, but at the time had no solid economic base on which the country could survive. Added to that was the extremely controversial manner in which West Papua was made part of Indonesia by the UN sanctioned "Act of Free Choice". Many of my wantoks (friends) from West Papua or PNG itself termed it "Act of No Choice" (which it in fact was). This travesty left Australia with a 760km land-border with a large expansionist potentially hostile neighbour. The reality maybe was a key motivator to mount a crash programme to get the place independent as soon as possible.

In two years, the mine had paid for itself and was already turning in quite a profit, even in its leaner times. I well remember the day we arrived! We were on the plane, a Fokker 27, heading to Bougainville when the captain announced that Phnom Penh in Cambodia had fallen — 17 April 1975.

The scenery was stunning, the road to the mine climbed over 1100 metres, with stunning views of the island and its active volcano, Mt Bagana. The clear sea and reef became a favourite place of mine. However, my multicultural development started here as well. We were living in Arawa at Section 5. Arawa was the major town on Bougainville set up only a few years before we arrived. Even at the young age of nine, I had local friends, but again at school I never seemed to get on well.

At Bovo Primary, the expatriate primary school in Arawa, the "grade hopscotch" resumed — back to Grade 2 then 3 then 4. Drew left Bougainville in 1977 to go to boarding school at St Peter's in Brisbane, where many of my future schoolmates from the Cape were at the time. There were more visits to experts in Australia regarding my problems at school, maybe five between 1976 and 1978, when Dad took his five-week annual leave. While Dad was on leave we did road trips — Brisbane to Cairns, Brisbane to Melbourne, etc. Of course, an attempt was made to steer me away from my local friends often by grounding me to the house. To me, the "Why can't you be like everyone else?" question was met by the fact that the "everyone else" they referred to were actually not on the higher moral plane that Mum thought they were. The reason was simple: I felt like many behaved like spoilt brats towards the locals and to any other person of polite manner. In fact, the locals knew them as BCL Brats! There was nothing worthy of imitating there, in my book.

Punishment was sure if I shook hands with any of the locals in my family's presence, especially from my elder brother. To this day I am unsure if this was racially motivated or the fact that they were being made the butt of jokes by their expatriate mates. With Dad, I am sure it was the latter, as he was not really a racist at heart.

There was another thing I was starting to pick up — the love of alcohol — but no one noticed it. This was a real indicator of just how far our family was slipping apart, even then. I was also forbidden to go out, as again my involvement with my local friends was not liked. With that start, the bullying and other problems at school and at home was the rich fertiliser that helped with the growth of that weed that became the huge tree of self-destruction. This had well and truly started when I went to St Barnabas in 1979 and the near total destruction that followed the remedy took twenty-five years to actually do. As for the relations between us brothers and the bullying — it is too much effort and a waste of scarce mental and spiritual resources to maintain a grudge. As a South African born Baptist Pastor remarked to me, 'The art of turning the 'I' in 'bitter' to the 'E' in 'better' is simple in writing but hard in life, but is an essential task that forms the reason why many Christians often behave towards others in a way that is anything but.

When I came home from boarding school, I returned with a toolbox with all sorts of stuff in it, courtesy of BCL. Dad told me never to talk about it. However, if a local was caught "organising" only a portion of that, he was sacked on the spot! When Dad left, he had lots of BCL stuff in his stores. I actually inherited some of it when he died and some of the BCL stuff is in my toolbox! Some expats even "organised" (as it could charitably be called) heavy equipment bulldozers and the like, and sequestered them in Australia to be used when they left the island.

Another thing was the hypocrisy. For example, many of the expats would talk badly about the locals and usually used generalised terms for things like break-ins, saying, 'They stole this and that.' Added to this, there was (like Exmouth) a remote large town in the middle of a nice but very unfamiliar setting. There were many divorces, usually because the bloke or the wife or both were having a fling with a member of the very same people they would say some derogatory things about, as in *Desperate Housewives*.

Overall it was a typical mining-town type setting; hard drinking and hardworking, where the smart ones (like my parents) saved all the pay they could to buy a house "down south" to live in when they left the job. Others were not so smart and often had real problems adjusting to life once they had gone back to Australia. Most rotated through the CRA mines in Australia and elsewhere.

Several things that formed cornerstones of my outlook on the world politically had their start on Bougainville. First, the reputation of the Fijian soldiers in WW2 when the island was occupied by Japan. The battle for Bougainville involved Fijian troops as part of the Commonwealth forces and they fought with high distinction, attracting admiration and respect. Second, the West Papua situation, as I met some people in Panguna who had fled Papua when the Indonesians took over and afterwards. At school in Ravenshoe, there was a young girl who had been in Tembagapura in Indonesian Papua and saw things she couldn't easily talk about. Third, interests, Melanesian politics and tactics. Fourth, geology. Fifth, aircraft.

My knowledge of PNG was very good, as was my knowledge of the political situation on Bougainville. For instance, the war started in 1988; I said it would start in 1984, and indeed, there were signs of it even in 1981. My timing of the place erupting was four years out but not inaccurate about the outcome. There were those expatriates that had strong links to the island who saw the train coming. However, they were often treated as pariahs that did not know what they were talking about. They were not regarded as good company by the other expats. Things were too good for an expatriate on Bougainville to have the truth about the political volcano they were working in raining on what was a very lucrative party!

However, the view was not shared by anyone with a cursory knowledge of the island; its people or its politics. Anyone with local friends, both Bougainvillean and Mainland PNG, knew the place had a veneer of calm. The completely tense environment was kept calm by often-frantic negotiations by both local and expatriate trouble-shooters and a few liaison officers. Often the "pariahs" mentioned earlier were on call to keep trouble at bay by assisting to defuse conflicts. Often they taken off their regular job at the mine because of the fact that they, like me, had an attitude that if you live in a place you get wantoks (local friends); if you don't, then go back to where you came from. They went back to their duties after the dispute was resolved. However, for their other job they were always on standby. Such people stalled the conflict for years. Therefore, what were the rest of the expatriates doing and what were those who were supposed to be checking on the place's stability doing when a oft-gated 12 year old kid knew the likely outcome still mystifies me to this day!

At the heart of most grievances regarding BCL was the fact that the agreements made in 1967 (The Bougainville Copper Act) had become dated and were not portable between the generations as a result. Policy was rigid in PNG regarding the mine and a younger generation was growing up who saw the inflexibility that resulted in what was a decent set of social responsibility programmes and payments in 1967 become eaten up by inflation, time, circumstances and unequal application they were fast becoming a joke.

Rebellions do not start in a vacuum of boredom; they start when all other avenues to get grievances addressed fail, when the governed are not listened to by those who govern. The cancerous thoughts then are given credibility by a perception that they are contributing but not receiving a just share of economic output. In addition, they see themselves often excluded from the full life of a nation they did not really want to be part of but being forced to contribute towards. Of course, the massive scar of the mine and Jaba River waste outflow which can be seen from space is another catalyst. I believe Bougainville was a war that could easily have been averted by a simple renegotiation of the agreement that underpinned the mines operations to get a more updated and equitable result for the landowners and other stakeholders. There was a great opportunity in 1976 to defuse the situation, but it was squandered.

When we left in 1982 I was forced to chose to leave in a family meeting. My father blamed me for him not getting another two years in at BCL as a result until literally the night he died in 1995.

Chapter 4

St Barnabas School Ravenshoe; A short time lasts a lifetime

In 1978, I was set on a path I should never have taken; first, to a school in Corinda, Brisbane, where I lasted a term and actually seriously injured someone by doing a completely stupid act. I jumped from a six-foot cement pipe onto another boy — not smart! I was simply not suited to be there. The assessors who had the smart idea about sending me there then recommended another place to my parents: Ravenshoe, a wind-swept place at 1100 metres, Qld's highest town. I commenced school there from 1979 at St Barnabas School, located on the eastern entrance to town set in what was quite a nice part of the world.

Of course, other than a prospectus, there was utterly nothing else regarding the school or its history for anyone to look at. However, a good gauge of how the place was is indicated by the way the Anglican school closed very suddenly in 1991. This indicates to me that the lawyers were not far off! Another indicator was that the archives of the school were dumped somewhere. Where that was depended upon whom you spoke to in the town; and St Barnabas' is "a fairly dirty piece of old town laundry". To my understanding, no one really wants to talk about that place, having myself attempted to do — and I still might do — a history on it.

Four years — a short time in fifty years — but traumatic

events often happen in only short periods. Vietnam veterans in America went on a two-year rotation; a short time. Sexual abuse, especially repeated sexual abuse, lasts only a short time, but it can pollute for a lifetime! I had a few Jewish friends who had survived World War 2, including an old Dutchman who had been in a concentration camp. On average, their stay in the camps was two to three years. For many of the refugees I was to meet later as well, the traumatic period was only a short time in their life, but it still affects them today. St Barnabas was my own version of the above. I had nightmares of being back there, and suffering multiple abuses, for twenty years after leaving.

The "grade hopscotch" had a final move: I jumped from Grade 5 to Grade 8! With what was going on around me I thought at first it would be OK, but within a week of my arriving, the true nature of the place dawned on me. Firstly, it was rainy; secondly, it was cold; thirdly, there were many bullies; fourthly, the staff ranged from concerned to apathetic.

There were three headmasters over my time there. First, there was Challan. He was a strict teacher but managed to keep control of the place reasonably well. Generally, he was quite concerned about the student's welfare. Secondly there was Mr Hurst, who was sacked after only one term. Then Challan's second in command, Fleming, took over in 1980. He was a decent Administrator and without him, I doubt that the place would have remained open even during my time. He was a man who did not mind the kids getting up to mischief a bit but that is where his good nature seemed to end. He had a very bad side to him too. He was seen by most as a racist, with a very nasty sense of humour, with draconian and collective punishments that were sometimes quite crass or downright filthy, which involved hard labour or cleaning out the grease trap outside the kitchen or to clean out the manure outfall. The Aboriginal kids and their friends often got these jobs (guess where that put me).

The church pastors were two men in the four years I was there. One later died in Africa, martyred I believe, and there were allegations of sexual abuse on his part, but I think neither would have done so. There were three members of staff who did have allegations of inappropriate behaviour levelled at them. There were two relationships between staff and Grade 12 kids that I know of from '79 to '82.

There was quite a turnover of teaching staff as well and any kid whose parents believed them about the state of the school and its toxic culture was not there very long. There were two kids from Bougainville, a young lady, and myself from Panguna where the BCL mine was. She of all people did not need to be immersed in an environment like that at St Barnabas. Frail and very quiet and preyed on even more than I was! She left at the end of 1979 and no other kids from Bougainville came to the school after that. The fact that my father probably recommended the place to her parents probably made for strained relations between my parents and other expats.

Some of the abuses at St Barnabas have recently emerged with the Royal Commission into Institutional Abuse that the Australian government had set up. In addition, what my parents were not told was that the school was a last port of call before the juvenile detention centre for many of its white boys. In short, it was low on the totem pole as far as reputation went. My time there was marked by bullying, other abuse, and a slowly deteriorating self-image. My view of God started with what I saw at the school and I ended up almost atheist. My outlook was more "agnostic" to put it better, as even then God had been there and the fact that my time there did not deteriorate even more to me was a sign that He was somewhere in the place.

In addition, I had made a decision to say the sinner's prayer and become a Christian in 1980. However, the place did not help anyone in any faith; rather its toxic environment made many an Atheist out of the kids who went there. The make-up of the place racially was that, out of about 104 kids, about forty were Aboriginal or Torres Strait Islander, four white kids from PNG, and the balance white kids from all over the Cape, like many of the Indigenous kids there. The racism was covert in the school but as I was to find out, a white boy who was from PNG and had a good relationship develop with the Islanders and Aboriginals there was almost at the bottom of the food chain.

The situation that emerged was where one had three brothers spread across the eastern seaboard of Australia leaving me totally isolated. However, it seemed as if my parents had at last solved the question of what to do with their youngest son. The first idea that emerged and stayed with me was that I was placed there in order to palm off the perceived problem. Besides, I was now with a school of white kids. To them the overwhelming number of PNG friends I had were no longer a problem. Whether the feeling was legitimate or not, it shaped my relations with the rest of my family for years afterwards. The feeling of being dumped in a very hostile place where one's very survival would turn out to be a miracle even though one was not yet eighteen! I think my parents were genuinely attempting to do the right thing in their choice of a boarding school but had not been able to do anything once it all started going sideways.

As part of the fact finding for this book, an attempt was made this year to get information as to why I ended up at St

Chapter 4

Barnabas and the file from the Child Guidence Institute in Brisbane not only told me that I had cognitive problems possibly from an accident when I was a baby, but also that they advised my parents to send me to Barnabas, knowing what it was and its reputation, but they did not mention more suitable similar possibilities such as Abergowrie or Trinity — all within 100km of Ravenshoe as the crow flies. I firmly believe that the fact that the alternatives were not raised sharply reduced my parents options with regards to school. This in my mind constituted a gross breach of duty of care on the part of the Qld Government assessors at the time towards both myself and my parents.

My dormitory was a good 500 yards across the flat from the school itself, and there were three steps to climb over the fences. Sometimes the farmer would put up electric fences and some boys would attempt to chase others — including me — into it. Therefore, we were the boys who ended up finding out how an electric fence worked and why. To avoid the fence, I had paced the distance out between it and the steps at either end of the paddock; that worked for a while but one night instead of hurdling the wire, I misjudged the distance, came down on the wire, and was booted seven feet or so. Running was the best option as walking was not a smart idea; if you wanted to stay unhurt, the bullies would be waiting in ambush in the paddock. There were actually three ways to get across the paddock for me, not just one, though it was a heavy breach of the rules not to keep to the path!

From 1980 onwards, I was relocated to Cedric House, which was actually on the main school campus, which solved the paddock problem but not the other problems I faced especially the bullying, which involved quite a lot of humiliating activities and a lot of abuse. One that was amusing to a few was the Dettol treatment, or pouring goanna oil liniment over one's underwear whilst one slept. One woke up and struggled to walk to the shower which was sometimes barred by one of the kids, and sometimes not. It gave the goose step a completely new meaning, as one started at an upright walk and as the pain increased, one started to adopt a bent over posture or waddle like a goose! There was quite a lot of abuse from fellow students that really acted to corrode my already low self-esteem of a nature so bad they can't be described here. Though there was support from some staff members and quite a few fellow students, the situation merely burned on until I left in 1982.

The schedule at the school ran as follows. First, there were classes all week, then on Friday afternoon the work detail. From Ravenshoe's red soil, our clothes were permanently stained. There were early morning runs (and another one if you were late on the scheduled one), breakfast, then church, then school, then sports, then dinner, then homework (called "Prep"), then finally at nine-thirty it was lights out. There was a dairy roster, with five kids being rotated through the milking time, for fourteen days each term per team, with seventy-two cows. I liked both digging the holes when gated which, as I had a smoking habit, was frequent. I also enjoyed working in the dairy, primarily because the digging built me up; it kept one steadily busy, even though you had been up at five am each morning. The meals were whatever the very resourceful cooks prepared. There was fresh meat, milk, etc. If you were punished the penalties took the shape of your weekends being spent digging holes, breaking rocks, weeding, or other such work.

There was a hierarchy of jobs where the mowing and machinery jobs went to the "pets" and the worst jobs went to those who were not liked or were not seen to be intelligent enough from the staff member's point of view. As said earlier, Mr Fleming's favourite for the "peasants" were the filthiest jobs. First, there was the manure outfall, where you were up to your waist in liquid manure, clearing it from the drain outfall. However, he had another favourite — "The Sump", the grease trap outside the kitchen. The headmaster let girls and boys do the job, so it was a very "equal opportunity"! You would stand in this putrid muck up to your waist, swilling this stuff out with a bucket into a wheelbarrow, then taking it up the back and tipping it.

I got that job, usually with the headmaster's sick sense of humour announcing my participation, and the two others who laughed first at my predicament. The result: a boy with his two worst enemies in "the same filthy boat". It was a punishment within a punishment within a punishment like a Russian Matrioshka doll. The first punishment was the job itself, the second punishment was the others steering clear of you because you stank for days, and the third punishment was because you would be attempting to mask the stench with whatever you could find (even girls' spray). You would then be a "Queenie" (homosexual) — not a good thing in a rural school in those days! One punishment by the school, and two in the mind of the leading kids in the place. One day I got my revenge, by slopping sump all over the headmaster's new moleskins "by accident" as he walked past. Though he screamed blue murder at me, I never got punished for it, though when I cleaned myself up I took care to get out of range of his hands for a week!

As mentioned earlier, I had made friends with many of the Aboriginal and Torres Strait kids especially. One of the Ambushers mentioned earlier who chased me into the electric fence was one of the leaders of the Aboriginal kids in the place and used to delight in his task! One night he stopped me and said, "You're not a racist like the others". He was the first of many Aboriginal and Islander kids who shook hands with me. Then a few others did as well. With the Torres Strait Islander, I used to get into trouble, because in PNG, the Australian border was drawn halfway between the tip of the Cape and the PNG mainland, with several of the Torres Strait Islands included as Western Province, not Australia. Yet the kids from there were Melanesian, not Aboriginal, and even some of the Aboriginal kids would not look out of place in Bougainville! I knew Pidgin and therefore managed to get quite a few friends there and a few white friends as well. However, in 1981, the group arrived from Drew's school and I was singled out for particular attention for a month until the newcomers discovered that I was not a racist and they could actually work quite well with me. Again, it is only very recently that I discovered why.

Though my parents were told about what was happening they did not believe me, that a place they paid 700 dollars a term for was slowly killing their son! How the story of the young girl from Panguna who was abruptly pulled out did not arouse any suspicions, I do not know. By 1981 I was smoking: read "anything"! The wild tobacco bushes were a ready supply as there was little cash. The best kept secret of my time there was how I'd been drinking anything that gave a buzz — usually the fermented product of the molasses used to feed the dairy cows, which I had found out about by accident. By 1981, I had attempted suicide twice there, and was actually almost hanged in 1981 by some boys down at the dairy that formed part of the property! They were going to make another attempt at that, or worse, but a tense peace prevailed instead. Many years later I found out why my "Unilateral declaration of Independence" I had planned (telling everybody to go to hell and take off if they tried it again) was never carried out — the Aboriginal kids had heard the white kids who did the job bragging about it and beat them senseless.

Another girl showed up at St Barnabas, a German girl who had been disabled in a motor accident. She, like the girl from Panguna was easy prey by the bullies and briefly became my girlfriend in the dying days of my time at Barnabas; we would be briefly engaged at Alice Springs in 1988 but it did not work out. There was another girl I was interested in but thought that she could end up with a target on her back if she went out with me. She never found out until 2011!

I left in 1982. I had already hatched a plan for open revolt if I came back in 1983, and that was ready. However, in the final planning of my contingency plan, which called for real mischief, the note came through that I was not returning. I think the main problem with St Barnabas was that the staff were often out of their depth in a cross-cultural situation that was not unusual in Northern Australia. The staff, especially Fleming, often used frustration as a default position for their inability to properly do a job, which they had not really been adequately equipped for in a social environment that was utterly toxic.

The reality is that often parents and others in authority steadfastly refuse to believe a child when they are told what is going on so far away from the home. It is dismissed as "kids' stuff" and one is told to get over it. I definitely was not believed in the least, though I told my parents what was going on. The choice I had at home though was far more limited than the open spaces and the ability to have friends with who I chose even in that place.

I will close this chapter by mentioning a few facts that are relevant. It's interesting how many times what Jesus said about living by the sword and dying by it have come prophetically true. I found out that one of the boys who attempted to hang me hanged himself a few years on. Then there was another bloke I met in Ravenshoe in 2012 and at first he did not recognise me but when he did he took off through the roadhouse and vanished just like that! To me it came down to stupid kids doing stupid things. The inability to forgive is one major factor that made the stress and pain last far more than it should have. For example, St Barnabas School was my first view of Qld and Australia. It took me twenty-five years to step back into Qld other than a few months in 1984-1985.

Chapter 5

Reasons to reject Christianity based on St Barnabas experiences, and why they are flawed

Before continuing on with the main thrust of this book, one must attempt to reconcile what has happened with the Bible I uphold as God's Word. Many of the excuses against Christianity I saw played out in the school which was an Anglican School and therefore should have been operating as much as possible within the rules and spirit of the Bible and the Christ they professed to uphold. The fact that they didn't set the stage for a lot of wrecked lives and a lot of students being pushed away from the Gospel. The statistics regarding atheism I tend to dispute. However if you had a statistic for the "cynical" then I think the overwhelming majority of the "atheists" would be reflected there.

As part of my target audience is the latter category, I would be doing a gross disservice to the reader if I didn't attempt to compare the excuses and reasons people are cynical. To do that, one needs to start with humankind's relationship with its Creator, then work out from there. Therefore, let's start with what the Bible says of humankind's position in relation to God and the chances of making it to heaven just as we are. The Bible is pretty straight to the point when it talks about the nature of the human race and Jesus' unique position regarding that condition.

1. "ALL have sinned and come short of the Glory of God." (Romans 3:23)

2. "For the wages of sin is death, but the free gift of God is eternal life in Christ Jesus our Lord." (Romans 6:23)

3. "However, God shows his love for us in that while we were still sinners, Christ died for us." (Romans 5:8)

4. "If you confess with your mouth that Jesus is Lord and believe in your heart that God raised him from the dead, you will be saved. For with the heart one believes and is justified, and with the mouth, one confesses and is saved." (Romans 10:9-10)

5. "Therefore, since we have been justified by faith, we have peace with God through our Lord Jesus Christ." (Romans 5:1)

Now, the excuses that I've often heard:

Excuse one: 'There's more than one way to heaven, all the religions lead to one spot.'

Except for one slight problem, Jesus repeatedly claimed not only a uniqueness but also Divinity. He took the throne above all others in a way that disqualified him from being a great teacher and prophet but only gave one choice: King of Kings and Lord of Lords.

1. "God said to Moses, 'I AM WHO I AM. This is what you are to say to the Israelites: I AM has sent me to you.'" (Exodus 3:14)

2. "Jesus answered, 'I am the way and the truth and the life. No one comes to the Father except through me.'" (John 14:6)

3. "'Very truly I tell you,' Jesus answered, 'Before Abraham was born, I am!'" (John 8:58)

4. "Who, being in very nature God, did not consider equality with God something to be used to his own advantage." (Philippians 2:6)

The I AM would have really got up the noses of any Jew listening to Him. I AM was and is a title for Yahweh, or Jehovah, which is the English translation of the name of God.

We are getting into an even bigger dilemma, that is, if all religions are their own way to the same place, either God is a schizophrenic and not worth His title or Jesus is who He says He is and therefore the suggestion that all roads lead to Rome is false.

Excuse two: 'I was at a church school or other institution and the priest and staff abused kids in many ways.'

Institutional abuse and abuse of office is the abrogation of duty of care imposed by the Lord as well as by the law of the land. However, it is often compounded by disbelief of those who tried to do the right thing but cannot believe their sincere efforts have gone bad because those they entrusted with their kids have let them down.

Well, Jesus had a lot to say about that. He made a warning that showed his views clearly:

"Jesus said, 'But whosoever shall offend one of these little ones which believe in me, it was better for him that a millstone was hanged about his neck, and that he was drowned in the depth of the sea.'" (Matthew 9:41)

Those who have a higher responsibility will face a higher level of judgement. Everyone wants to rule the world. There is a hit from *Tears for Fears* titled that and it is true. It is no different in the Church, and many splits in the local church are often because of ambition rather than a major departure from biblical doctrine on part of the parent church.

However, I have a heavy caution regarding this: being "the boss" also means the responsibility rests with them more than anyone else does. Even they are accountable, in fact more so. A few verses on this:

1. "Let not many of you become teachers, my brethren, knowing that as such we will incur a stricter judgment." (James 3:1)

2. "But the one who did not know it, and committed deeds worthy of a flogging will receive but few. From everyone who has been given much, much will be required; and to whom they entrusted much, of him they will ask even more." (Luke 12:48)

3. "Not everyone who says to me, 'Lord, Lord,' shall enter the kingdom of heaven, but he who does the will of My Father in heaven. Many will say to me in that day, 'Lord, Lord, have we not prophesied in your name, cast out demons in your name, and done many

wonders in your name?' I will declare to them, 'I never knew you; depart from me, you who practice lawlessness!" (Matthew 7:21-23)

4. "Nothing in all creation is hidden from God's sight; everything is uncovered and exposed before the eyes of Him to whom we must give account." (Hebrews 4:13)

Those four verses are powerful enough; the third one makes everyone stop in their tracks, and if it does not then their hearts are hardened beyond listening. How many will face Hell because they sent innocent kids down the road to Hell by their actions and weak pathetic justifications? The fourth one you can see happening as abuse is investigated in several countries with celebrities, politicians and church officials all bought to justice as God refines His Church and delivers justice in a public way.

Excuse three: 'The Bible is racist.'
OK, a formula: Indigenous people + church or institutional abuse = this excuse. Remember at Barnabas many of the Aboriginal kids came as Christians and left with that totally gone.

Well, Racism had a lot to do with it and history is against the organised church, which needs to reconcile and confess its often-dark past in this regard. A quick look at many of Africa's worst leaders will clearly demonstrate that the way they were treated by so-called "Christian" institutions had a lot to do with the reason why they walked away from Christianity. Their countries often become a byword for all the wrong reasons because of their later leadership.

To examine the roots of the above history, a swift look at

mankind's point of view according to a world famous evolutionist is needed, then this cross-referenced with a look at the Bible's word on it and church history. "Is God racist?" is the blunt question, is it not?

There are several reasons why I have never believed in evolution even before I became a Christian. Biological reasons and the estimates of guesstimates that are so much part of evolutionary theory are a major part. A theory is not fact but it was the racism that emerged from it which is the main reason. Firstly, the full title of Charles Darwin's most famous contribution to history says it all: *"Origin of the Species and the triumph of the FAVOURED RACES in the struggle for life"* gives one a fairly good idea where he is coming from right there.

The Aboriginals were in fact "outed" by Charles Darwin as an inferior stage of evolution as were the Terra Del Fuegans on South America in his book *The Descent of Man* where he lumps Aboriginals in with gorillas.[1] In fact, there were Aboriginal remains in quite a few universities in Europe and Aboriginal people were often examined after their death by the scientists of the day because the missing link concept seemed to apply.

This rationale was legion in Australia and in fact, in Western Australia the term Rock Ape was coined to refer to Aboriginals. It's one of the worst insults to fire at an Aboriginal person in Australia. Even in the 80s and 90s, the rationale of Darwin was popular urban myth and belief in many parts of Australia. Of course, the apogee of this thinking was when Adolf Hitler wrote *Mein Kampf.*

As part of my undergraduate studies, I studied evolution at Charles Darwin University (previously NTU) in 1992 and

---

1 Darwin ;C;(1871) The Descent of Man p.521

failed it twice. The reason was that I could easily make sense of an argument even when it is hostile to my own if it has a basis in fact and place. I could not believe a word that was written by the evolutionists. As well as that, I found their own texts were often at odds with each other or an educated guess or downright fraudulent.

To illustrate the point above, Steven J Gould, one of the high priests of the subject, described a few classical "examples" of evolution such as the "Salamander to human" diagram that a thinker named Ernst Hankel drew and still is taught as academic murder.[2]

Anyone who uses Christianity as an excuse for racial theories may like to see what the Bible says, rather than what the talk of many mouths has to say about race. Arguments that base racism on Biblical verses are often taking the verses out of context or out of the surrounding verses.

Let us have a look at the situation from God's perspective:

Fact: God created all men in His image (Genesis 1:27).

Fact: All are sinners and come short of His Glory (Romans 3:23).

Fact: Each was created in its own kind (Genesis 7:5-9).

Fact: The Ethiopian Orthodox Church is the world's oldest established church, taking its documented lineage back to the Eunuch that Phillip met (Acts 8:27). The Egyptian Coptic Church is the second oldest. The Roman Catholic Church dates from the 4th Century not from the 1st. That was when Emperor Constantine made Christianity legal in the Roman Empire.

---

2 See Leigh.D (2012) "Black Magic, things you might not know about Evolution" at http://deadlybutterflies.blogspot.com.au/2012/06/things-you-may-not-know-about-evolution.html

I think the above is enough to put to bed that God loves everyone and favours no one. One rule is applied for all: Jew or Gentile, black or white or Asian. No matter who you are or where you are.

Excuse four: 'Women in the Church are less regarded than men.'

Here are some verses that seem to back that up and are often used against Christianity by critics. 1 Corinthians 14:35 says "Women should remain silent in the churches. They are not allowed to speak, but must be in submission, as the law says. If they want to inquire about something, they should ask their own husbands at home; for it is disgraceful for a woman to speak in the church." Also, "Wives, submit yourselves to your own husbands as you do to the Lord. For the husband is the head of the wife as Christ is the head of the church, his body, of which he is the Saviour. Now as the church submits to Christ, so also wives should submit to their husbands in everything." (Ephesians 5:22)

OK, any research of the New or Old Testament will find women are heroes of the faith. For a start, there is an entire Old Testament book dedicated to Esther, the queen who risked her life to save her nation. Then you soon find others such as Ruth, Rahab, Pharaoh's daughter who rescued Moses, Deborah (who was both prophet and judge as well as military leader in Judges), and Rizpah who protested a massacre (2 Samuel 21:10). In the New Testament there are many women in high leadership in the Church; Mary of course, the mother of Jesus. Think of the cultural context! Martha, the sister of Lazarus, held high position and respect in Jesus' inner circle. Tabitha, a seamstress and philanthropist (Acts 36-43) who Peter raised from the dead. Junia, referred to as an apostle by Paul in Romans 16:7, whose office was held in high esteem even a couple of hundred years later by other church leaders [3].

I have just taken half an hour of research at two am in the morning to refute this excuse! However, my last swipe at excuses used to justify subjugation of women is this one: Remember Ephesians "Wives submit to their husbands." Well, it has a follow up verse that a lot of men choose not to read because it means husband and wife are equal and must submit to each other and places a high obligation of protection on the husband. "Husbands, love your wives, just as Christ loved the church and gave himself up for her (Ephesians 5:24). Wow, what can I say? Christ died for His Church! Therefore, according to the Bible, that and nothing less is the level of commitment a man should have with his wife in Scripture.

Yes, I am the first to admit that the church has a lot to answer for by perverting the meaning of the very word it stands on!

---

[3] Evans R. (2012) "Who's who amongst Biblical Women Leaders" at; https://rachelheldevans.com/blog/mutuality-women-leaders

Chapter 6

Alice Springs and a rough start to adulthood!

In 1982, we moved to Beenleigh on the south side of Brisbane where my parents had bought a house in Adelaide Circuit. Since I had now left school, looking for work was a pre-occupation. Drew found work quickly and me, well, it took a lot longer. I had a girlfriend in Inala but our relationship was strained and being on the dole, I was becoming fed up and decided to go to Alice Springs on the invitation of a schoolmate. It was a town where I would live from 1983 until 1992, a town that I was happy to be in. Now, the restrictions on smoking and drinking, which were still carefully hidden from my parents, were gone!

With independence, suddenly the controls that kept the lid on my hidden life were suddenly not there. Three things really took off from day one. The first was my drinking, the second was fighting, third was very loose living — wine, women, and song — topped off with going in and out of police cells. Any hope of getting an order in my life swiftly unravelled in spite of some help from people at the Salvation Army where I was living and a few jobs that I'd managed to get.

In late 1983, I had a fight with a white bloke, walked to the town's council chambers and was met by a man from the Potter's House, a Pentecostal church. He said, 'Hello, Keith!' He did not know me at all! It was my decision to accept the

Lord Jesus as my personal Lord and Saviour at the Potter's House in Alice Springs in 1983.

The Salvation Army in Stuart Terrace was a single men's hostel. I lived between there and the Todd Riverbed drinking with my Aboriginal friends and getting up to all sorts of rather stupid things. During my time at the Salvos, I was a seventeen-year-old man lumped in with many ex-cons and others who were also giving me a few problems, but not all. However, the decision was made because what happened at school was not going to happen again in my view; 'If they couldn't be sensible, I'd make them scared'. Therefore, anything that could cause injury became my way to settling arguments. Though I'd threatened several with knives on different occasions, I never actually caused injury to anyone there. Quite a few would call me names reserved for white men who hung around the Aboriginal people. However, the same dynamics I saw in Bougainville were also at play in this case as many of the men in the hostel drank and fornicated with the very same people I was doing it with. I often attempted to defend the woman I was with from these same blokes who were talking in racist terms about the Aboriginals when in the hostel.

As far as authority there was concerned, one had a Captain and an Envoy. The Envoy was a big bloke who had been through many things in his life. However, like many in Alice, he was racist. He was also not afraid to use his fists on anyone who needed them to be used on, me included in many ways. A lot of these blokes simply didn't understand any other language and a show of force was usually administered once or twice before they were evicted.

He had been in Qld and in WA at Katanning from what I found out. Katanning, like St Barnabas', featured in the

Institutional Abuse Royal Commission for all the wrong reasons. Again, attempts to actually research what the Salvos did there was greeted like my sniffing about was greeted in Ravenshoe. Again, the way one was being treated, and seeing others treated that way, was fast influencing what I thought of the church. I went there for ten months in and out, then four months on my return from Darwin in 1986.

My progress was stuck in a netherworld — Todd River and its environment. I was only able to get manual jobs; no one would employ or have time for a white youth living in and out of the Todd River and the town camps. An environment sucks one in and holds one in it regardless of who you are, what race you are, or your status in life. It all ended up in the Todd River, which was the great equaliser of status. The Todd Riverbed and town camps could accurately be described as a classless society; whatever you thought was simply dissolved in it. The Darwin counterpart, known as the "Long Grass" was no different. People from all occupations ended up there. It was where I lived when I was in Darwin in 1984 and again in 1985. There was one fact though. That type of environment got you into trouble with everyone and often killed those in it swiftly if they were not able to cope, and like a boa constrictor it squeezed the life out of you if you were strong enough to survive. That is what you ended up doing; surviving as a prisoner of your surrounds and of your own making.

At that time I'd nearly been killed three times and in two cases it was only God who stopped my death! First was when a bloke threw a flagon at me and hit the back of my head after a drunken fight. It resulted in a depression at the back of my skull. Second was when I got into a fight and was belted to within an inch of my life. The police didn't think very highly of the way my drunken mouth abused them either, which lead to a few instances where the "Ways and Means Act" was applied. Third was my suicidal thoughts of deliberately walking up to a drunken bloke twice my size and starting a fight. In this, one took no notice of one's injuries unless one was bleeding. You just woke up, sobered up and got up, dusted yourself off, and restarted your day. Of course, the police were overall quite racist except for a few who stuck up for me when their colleagues were about to give me an often well-deserved hiding. Often when you were locked up they would make loud noises when you woke up hungover. That lasted until a nurse told me that hangovers were caused by dehydration. Therefore, before I went to sleep in the cell I'd drink quite a lot of water. As a result, the police game lost its fun.

One day I had gotten smart with the police arresting me and they decided to attempt to blast my remaining sanity to smithereens by teaching me a lesson. They put me in a cell below a nutter who just sang 'Tra la la, tra la la, la la la' repeatedly. My mates and I in the drunk tank were being driven mad. We swapped stories as to exactly how we were going to teach him a lesson when we got out, but the police released him about half an hour early. We never found out who it was.

In fact, one day under Stott Terrace bridge (the main Todd River Crossing), the police told me I shouldn't worry about any future as I'd be dead at thirty. I was utterly determined to live that down and if one could see where one of the turning points of my story was, it's when I was told this. I forgot who said it until recently when a former Attorney General in the NT, an ex-police officer, told me he remembered telling me that. This is one bloke who has a great thanks to who was a very controversial AG for his words ! I returned to Beenleigh in late 1984 and returned to Alice in 1985 after finding no work there. Besides, my view of Qld was still very bad. Upon my return to Alice Springs I found work at the Mia Pizza Bar and a no nonsense Italian family began to train me. They were the third Italian employer I had in Alice to date. Yes I was drunk, but yes I was attempting to get off the bottle and was hard working, and hardworking is what mattered to those people. I was staying at the Anglican Lodge in Bath Street and generally my life started to settle down and improve. My commitment to Christ was reasonably stable. That said, other than my Todd River mates, the crowd at Potters House, and the people who I worked for up to date I had no friends outside that circle. Add to that I felt that no one really understood what I had been through whether in Qld or in the NT to date.

Between April and September 1985 things were stable and I was living fairly well and staying out of trouble. I was back at Potters House. I used to ride a bicycle and would ride up to fifteen kilometres out of town. My relationship with the local Aboriginal folk was generally good, and I was outreaching them for the church. The result was that the church was eighty per cent Aboriginal by September. However, the controlling environment and lack of any proper compassion and abundance of legalism had me seriously start to question why I was at Potters anyway. I had found more work, however things were going to start heading south again. This started when a thirty two-year-old woman named Kummanjayi Inkamala with four kids came into my life after I'd helped her disarm her husband who was beating her up. He had stabbed her a month earlier and had a knife wound in her stomach was clearly visible. She left in late August for Darwin. I followed her north on the 21st of September.

I arrived in Darwin and stayed initially at the Salvation

Army Hostel in Mitchell Street. Then I ended up in the parks and reserves (the "Long Grass") for a while. Unknown to me at the time, Kumanjayi had another boyfriend there. I had unwittingly strode into that completely ignorant of the fact. He had quite a large family and I was in and out of the so-called "Long Grass" and being in more and more trouble with his people, his family from Arnhem Land. A "war" started, principally over my relationship with a woman thirteen years my senior, who lived and drank in Darwin whilst her four kids were being looked after by her sister, who I think was overworked and overstressed. I put many a foot wrong with her long suffering sister in Alice Springs and as well as the people Kyumanjayi was with in Darwin

Attempts to set up properly failed repeatedly and my own personal security was very uncertain as things rapidly deteriorated as I started making mistake after mistake and started tripping over traditional things I had no business tripping over. Again, I attempted to go to Potters House in Darwin but that failed. I restarted smoking and was drinking down at Humpty Doo fifty kilometres out of town.

After several threats were made and my own ability to stay in Darwin being undermined one of the family there, I hurriedly packed my things into a big metal box and exited Darwin on the 31st of December 1985. I was so worried that the local Top End mob would get me that I stayed on the bus until Elliott, which is where the desert meets Top End savannah country 760 km south of Darwin. I later discovered that there were plans to inflict payback on me. Sure, I had broken their law, and secondly, I had wrecked camps in my attempt to retaliate for grievances real and imagined. The start of the realisation that there were just too many enemies made and way too much done by either them or me began to surface when I stumbled across a white bloke who had been stoned with rocks in front of the Uniting Church.

There are a lot of urban myths about why people end up in the "Long Grass". Well, the "Long Grass" is often populated by people who are highly intelligent but for some reason had their lives completely derailed. Kumanjayi's other boyfriend was no exception. If I could mark the point where I realised that I could not get peace if I kept the relationship with Kumanjayi and that the hostile relationship with her other bloke was not warranted, it was the day when I had a good conversation with her boyfriend in Darwin who was sober at the time. He was formerly a teacher in Milingimbi, but as many do, he eventually burned out and joined that egalitarian class known as the "Long Grassers". Therefore, I wanted to make peace and gracefully bow out of Darwin. However, too many things were said and done to do that. I left without making peace with a man who had gained my respect. Even though I was angry with him for years, the respect never wavered. He died in 1989.

My commitment to Christ was always under pressure in Darwin but when I returned to Alice Springs and tried to pick up the pieces, a battle was being waged. I wanted to prove that copper wrong, wanted to get off the bottle, wanted out of the environment I was in. In spite of what she did in Darwin and did not tell me, I still loved and sympathised with Kumanjayi and her family. I wanted her to be like me and we could jointly take on and win over the bottle and the deadly lifestyle that caused so much misery for both of us. She returned to Alice and we attempted to pick up where we left off.

We lived at Namatjira Camp near the old Abattoir. I was often the only sober bloke there and was often stopping fights. The fact that I was starting to rebel against the lifestyle I found myself in and attempted to recommit my life to Christ placed strain on my relationship with Kumanjayi who loved me but couldn't make a break with what was holding her down. I even thought of taking them all to Carnarvon in WA but did not have any money to facilitate that move. We separated, though we still loved each other dearly for years afterwards.

Chapter 7

Is there life after Alice Springs?

Of course, my attempts to climb out of the situation I was in was always faced with the same dilemma as far as employment was concerned. In a town like Alice, anyone who had the friends I did and the relationships I had held little prospect for decent employment. No one had time for someone who had one foot in the Todd Riverbed and the other in the white community! Alice Springs was, and is, a very racially-charged place, even these days. This is never far below the surface there.

Therefore, I worked in menial jobs, some of which, in fact, were quite disgusting! They would make the sump at Barnabas look like a rose garden. There was my ongoing battle with the alcohol and getting above my dead-end lifestyle that was by now killing my friends at the rate of one every three months. Another decision I made was to leave Potters House. It was getting harder and harder to stay in it. For instance, every time someone did something, the pastor was "the boss" and had to know about it. The church was one big "revolving door", with the congregation always "backsliding" as they put it. Taking jobs out bush was "verboten", as was having a TV, and if you did not pay your tithes they would follow you up. The end of my involvement with that church came swiftly. When I came back from Darwin, I mostly stopped attending, and after March I stopped altogether.

The effort to get things on a better footing collapsed like a house of cards within two months. I was working at the Town Council fixing footpaths and my drinking resumed. My pattern was always shotgun drinking. That is, you slammed as many down as you could to get drunk then slowed down to keep yourself drunk. The fighting was resuming, the old life of girls resumed too.

In 1986 I was arrested several times on charges ranging from fighting to bad-mouthing police and in late 1986 Escape Lawful Custody was added to the list. Yes, I know what it is like to be beaten up by the police, but in all honesty I reckon that, had I kept my mouth shut, it would not have happened as often as it did. There was one policeman who liked to fine me for anything, and another who used to call me all sorts of names, usually those reserved for white blokes with Aboriginal women, terms which thankfully I rarely hear today.

In November 1986, I got a Housing Commission place in Bath Street, a one-bedroom flat. Once again, I attempted to recommit my life to Christ. The same pizza bar that employed me in 1985 did so again and I worked with them until September 1987. However, in late 1987 I started to get into serious trouble with the police, especially after several incidents involving men dragging women into the Todd River. I hit several people with the heavy chain I used to lock up my bike over time. My logic then, and now, is that they should respect women! Yes, violence is not the best way to solve problems but there are a few who, just like in the hostel in Alice Springs, refused to listen to any other language.

For the rest of the 1980s I lived there. For three years I was doing OK, then from 1988 to 1991 my life started the downward spiral again — drinking ouzo and other things, and the familiar pattern that was a part of my life when God had a back seat. I worked for a gardener in Alice named Geoff Miers, a real blessing. Sure, like my Italian bosses he wanted you to be professional, but he was a good teacher for what was a very unruly pupil! As well as him there were a few others. I was also finding work at a scrapyard. I thought, 'Well, we aren't going to get any better, and we could be doing far worse.' I became a prolific letter-writer to the newspaper, both the NT News and the Centralian Advocate. I once confronted some anti-Pine Gap protesters; they would come up from all-points south about the US spy base at Pine Gap and cry wolf as to how it was a nuclear target. I told them that there was as much of a chance of Alice Springs — a town that has a dry-riverbed regatta called the "Henley on Todd" and where the river flowed only a handful of days a year — being attacked as there was of a high tide there! Of course, after that there was a flood of letters to the Advocate about that, a lot of them calling me things indescribable here. Well, we are still here, Pine Gap is still there, and Alice is still 1300 kilometres away from the nearest beach! Point made!

There was my ongoing life that seemed to settle in to a plain of bad living, but on the whole, reasonably peaceful and often drunk living. Alcohol had its grip on me again and though I only drank in the afternoon when I get home it was still a major problem. I had given up trying to give up smoking; a habit I had since 1985 with a month break in 1986. Yes it was not healthy, yes it was a monumental waste of money, and for a man who was attempting to recommit himself to Christ it was a disgraceful waste of His resources. Jesus obviously took notice of my prayers because in late June 1991, the twenty cigarette a day habit suddenly ended. I thought I was stuck with it and that was that. However, within a week

I was a non-smoker! Then the alcohol stopped; again, this was suddenly.

However, in 1991 there were also signs that my time was ending in Alice. For a start, my traditional sources of work were drying up; my boss at the local recyclers was one of the victims of Keating's "recession we had to have", and he shut down in April. Then in October, I was called into the Housing Commission's office and told that I was tampering with the gas pipes that fed our flats hot water system. This was false, and had I known what I know now, it would have been challenged. However unlike then the NT now has a Residential Tenancies Act. That's why I ended up in Liana Court; a filthy bedsitter in a three-storey block of former Health Department buildings, listening to a drunken rendition of 'Bimbo, bimbo, where we going to go-eyo?' from upstairs at four am in the morning!

I reckon the Housing Commission were sick of me going over their heads to the Minister. They were sick of the escalating violence inflicted on their flat as my alcoholic ways again took hold; and sick of a steadily rising pattern of complaints coming from the neighbours. The fact that by the time they made up their mind to do something about me the alcohol and other problems subsided must have come too late. After a fight, my last as a drunk, the gang I was fighting with smashed the windows. To the Housing Commission that was the last straw, and I was on my way to Liana Court and "Bimbo" whether I liked it or not. I reckon even God must have thought that Keith needed a shock! I wanted a transfer — well, I got one! Simpson's Gap was a nice sleeping spot for me! I loved long-distance rides, often going up to 140 km from town; usually, though, I went about 10 km out most times.

On the 21st of November 1991 news had arrived of Kummanjayi Inkamala's death and we had her funeral in

Chapter 7

Hermannsburg. After that, I decided to get serious about Christ. I would not expect much from Him. There were several reasons for this state of mind. The fact that I'd walked away from Him years before; secondly, my view of Jesus was that of a strict schoolmaster, taking things away from us, and the Holy Spirit was like one of the worst police in Alice Springs, ready to pounce at a moment's notice on anything that displeased him. This was my first teaching about Jesus, courtesy of the local Potter's House, where I had given my life to Jesus initially in 1983. It was this Jesus that I had resigned myself to having as my Lord again, "knowing" what He was like, and how He "dealt the cards". There was a huge gap between the Jesus I knew and the Jesus in the Bible. One would not disappear for years afterwards.

However, I preferred a future with Christ to a short future without Him if I had remained where I was and whom I remained with. I was halfway between Alice Springs and Ntaria riding my bicycle when I recommitted my life to Christ. As if a bankrupt with utterly no way out I decided that a chance of life with Jesus trumped a return to the "culture" I knew would see me killed like many of my friends were killed within a short time. The offer was a simple choice between turn and repent of your ways or burn; keep going and see where your folly will take you. I had decided to leave Alice Springs and move up to Darwin. Three problems — no, actually four — beset me. First, I had a Housing Commission flat in Alice Springs; second, I had no money for the bus fare to Darwin; third, I had low Grade 10 scores in Maths and other subjects. That meant that I had to pass an exam to be considered. My position being what it was if I didn't pass then it would mean sudden death to my chances in Darwin. My goal was to stay out of the Long Grass and keep the hard won peace.

After a week in Ntaria, I rode back to Alice on my trusty pushbike, which also had a homemade trailer (not used this time around) and sat the test. I passed for a Bachelor of Arts-type course and enrolled at NTU to commence in 1992. I spent what would be my last Christmas in Alice actually on the road to Hermannsburg. I remember the radio that was on the front of my pushbike announcing Gorbachev's ending of the USSR.

My major concerns were, how was I going to get to Darwin, and once I was there, where would I live? The departure date was set at the 20th of January 1992. The date got closer and closer, but something told me it would be OK. Therefore, I relied upon that "Thing", namely the Holy Spirit, who I began to see as a Person, a very stern and heavy-handed person, but a person who could be trusted to bring some order to a situation that was anything but orderly.

To demonstrate how apprehensive I was regarding coming to Darwin, I need to go back in time a bit. In 1990, I had worked in the RSPCA when they were refurbishing their facility in Berrimah, a suburb of Darwin. The problem was a lot of the gang who I was fighting with in 1985 had long memories. An opposition member who knew my boss well urged my employer to keep me in Alice for my own safety! Actually, what did happen was that I did go up to Darwin and I did the work at RSPCA and everybody, including me, kept the peace! It was the first indication that my question 'Is there life after Alice Springs?' was getting an answer.

In January, two things happened which were quite stunning at the time. First, my ticket up to Darwin was paid; second, I had fifty dollars spending money, via a letter that had been lost for months showing up on the day I left Alice! Third, I managed to get a place in the Salvos in Mitchell Street Darwin. The stage was set for my time in Darwin part 2.0!

Chapter 8

Asking the impossible, 'Are you ready?'

I read a book called *Winning Impossible Wars* by Col Stringer; I was possibly his last customer of his fishing gear shop when he first went into ministry and this was his first book. I was in the "Long Grass" when I first started to read this. OK, I was starting from an impossible position in human terms and about to embark on a programme that, without my commitment to Jesus Christ, was dead before it started.

To start the section, here is a look at what I thought of the Father, Son and Holy Ghost from 1979 to 1994 or thereabouts:

I had the view that Jesus was a teacher in the strict disciplinarian mould and the Holy Spirit was a spiritual equivalent of the worst copper I knew and God was a father, but not Abba Father; I knew him as Judge. I knew that with them, there was order, peace, but any revelation of love and fatherhood was absent.

Was my view the right view? Does the Bible contradict me? Let us have a look; these are a few verses of the Bible to ponder:

1. As a man so He becomes a valid choice to the human race (subject to exactly the same things as us). John 1:14 reads, "And the Word became flesh, and dwelt among us, and we saw His glory, glory as of the only begotten from the Father, full of grace and truth."

2. As God; Hebrews 1:8 says, "But of the Son He says, 'Your throne, O God, is forever and ever, and the righteous sceptre is the sceptre of his kingdom.'" Also, see John 14:6, "Jesus answered, 'I am the way and the truth and the life. No one comes to the Father except through me.'"

3. Mankind's nature barred him from heaven and God. Romans 3:23; "For all have sinned and come short of the Glory of God."

4. His love for mankind. John 3:16; "For God so loved the world He gave His only begotten Son for so whoever believes in Him..." (that is, stubbornly stands by him and His Word rather than merely believing He exists/existed) "...shall not perish but have eternal life."

5. His loyalty to Man. Hebrews 13:5; "Keep yourselves free of the love of money and be content with your lot for I will never leave you or forsake you."

Just those verses were sufficient enough to overturn my warped theology.

OK, on God and His nature as a Father:

1. Romans 8:15; "The Spirit you received does not make you slaves, so that you live in fear again; rather, the Spirit you received brought about your adoption to sonship. In addition, by him we cry, 'Abba, Father.'"

2. The Bible does not mean or refer to a 70s Swedish band by that name of course, but to a term in Aramaic

which translated means Father, or simply Dad, a child/father relationship that is not present in any other religion.

3. Matthew 7:9-11; "Which of you, if your son asks for bread, will give him a stone? Alternatively, if he asks for a fish, will give him a snake? If you, then, though you are evil, know how to give good gifts to your children, how much more will your Father in heaven give good gifts to those who ask him?"

4. James 1:27; "Religion that God our Father accepts as pure and faultless is this: to look after orphans and widows in their distress and to keep oneself from being polluted by the world."

5. Hebrews 12:7; "Endure hardship as discipline; God is treating you as his children. For what children who are loved are not disciplined by their father?"

On the Holy Spirit. He is a person not a "The"!

1. Romans 15:13; "May the God of hope fill you with all joy and peace as you trust in him, so that you may overflow with hope by the power of the Holy Spirit."

2. Titus 3:5; "He saved us, not because of righteous things we had done, but because of his mercy. He saved us through the washing of rebirth and renewal by the Holy Spirit."

3. Galatians 5:22-23; "But the fruit of the Spirit is love,

joy, peace, forbearance, kindness, goodness, faithfulness, gentleness and self-control. Against such things, there is no law."

4. Corinthians 13:14; "May the grace of the Lord Jesus Christ, and the love of God, and the fellowship of the Holy Spirit be with you all."

Yes, God is not mocked (Galatians 6:7) and Jesus is a judge (Acts 10:42). He commanded us to preach to the people and to testify that he is the one whom God appointed as judge of the living and the dead. However, He is not the stern taskmaster I thought he was and if you have that view, I reckon it's time you loved Him as a Father, respected Him as a judge, and know that He loves you.

Questions 4 U

1. Do you ever feel as if you are unable to get a start in life? Why? Do you think the Jesus you read about here can assist in your situation?

2. What's your view of church? Do you share the same views I did when I was in Alice Springs about God, Jesus and the Holy Spirit, or the church in general?

3. Do you attend Alcoholics Anonymous or a related group? If so, then do you base your rehabilitation plan on the 12 steps? If you are not a Christian, then do you think Jesus will help you to recover from the bounds of alcoholism and drug dependence and put your life back together?

Gloria my second eldest and me in Ba Fiji

Kathleen my youngest daughter and me in Fiji

Kathy and her mum at Lautoka 2015

Kathy, Watiqu and Nelson (2009)

Our house in Exmouth WA when I was 7 in 1973 photo taken in 2017

Me at lighthouse overlooking tower zero Exmouth WA. Tower Zero (back ground) is about 350 m tall and was the tallest structure in the Southern Hemisphere for many years

This is St Barnabas School in Racenshoe NQ, the office was the red brick building. Since the State Govt took it over a lot of buildings have been added such as the building to the left of the office.

This is Noel Acom and me at Lockhart River.

Me and David Claudie, ex schoolie from St Barnabas at his outstation at Wenlock River Qld.

At the tip of Cape York

Cape York Road

This bridge is one of my camp spots. It's where the copper told me I'd never live till 30.

Adi Lewa, my Hilux has gone right around Australia several times. She is extremely reliable. Here she is with a sign on the Tanami Road. This sign is not a gimmick for tourists — be prepared if you go bush!

The bicycle and home made trailer was known as the "Funny bike" to all the Indigenous kids wherever I went. Before I was driving it was my prime form of transport and it was the work horse in Elliott if the car broke down Its cargo has included kids, large Fijian Soldiers and whole pallets of cargo. The food on it is destined for Elliott. I could get food in Darwin and send it down cheaper than one could buy it in Elliott despite the place being on the Stuart Highway.

Graduation 2014 — I have two uni degrees, one in Sociology, Politics and History, the other a Bachelor of Laws.

First train to Darwin stops in Tennant Creek January 2004. I was just passing through Tennant Creek at the time and ended up all over the TV apparently!

Elliott NT where I was married and lived for 7 years, the hotel is in the foreground the Ampol has been demolished and the Elliott Mobil is in the back ground. the Stuart Highway is to the left.

Our house was where the car in the yard is at the end of this street in Gurungu North Elliott

We then moved to this house in Marlinja. The house opposite was built on rock and the foundation still twisted and cracked and the water supply was very unreliable. Even in Fiji I had reliable water even after Cyclone Winston tore the place up ! this is the norm sadly in many communities rather the exception

The end of the blockade, my first refuelling in Elliott after 2 years. I was seperated from my wife 7 months later.

Isiah when we were collecting wood out in the bush Elliott. 2010

Flooded Newcastle River taken in 2010. Compare the dry river photo beneath.

Humour — they reckoned that me and Rups looked similar, well if the shirt fits...almost wear it.

Kathy and me and a friend in Suva

Table under which we sheltered in cyclone Winston Fiji 2016. The crack in the table was where some roofing fell... my head was about 2 inches under the crack !

Raki Road

The aftermath of Cyclone Winston.

Myself, Sulia, her daughter and Amani in Vatusekiyasawa Fiji, a few days before Cyclone Winston (Cat 5) hit in 2016.

Vasiti, Junior and Myself in whats left of Vasitis house after Cyclone Winston hit Fiji, 320 km/hr winds made reinforced concrete walls shake like plywood My report to the NT News in Darwin was possibly the very first out of Raki Raki.

Part 2

Chapter 9

Restart in Darwin

Several miracles happened on my return to Darwin. The first was in the accommodation scene. Secondly, though my record with the Housing Commission being the way it was, this did not stop the transfer between centres being granted and a one bedroom flat becoming available in a city where there was an eight year waiting list at the time.

What motivated me to study at university? For a start, the way things ended up with me and what I saw in Alice had seen me critically examine the situation that afflicts many Aboriginal communities in this country, as well as many non-Aboriginal ones. While most people judge the depressing story around Australia's Indigenous people in the current tense, with what the case is now and the billions of dollars wasted on schemes that were flawed from word go, I was examining the *why*?

What lead to this situation where the people are purportedly "Land rich but dirt poor?" Why did many talented Aboriginal leaders end up on our streets and in the "Long Grass" and places like it and die before they are due? Why did the policies regarding Aboriginal people seem to produce nothing in spite of the billions of dollars ploughed into them over the years?

Yes, some of these questions could be answered through prayer, I firmly believe that. However, there are others that can only be answered by solid research and to look at the often painful past Australia has had and how to address the situation where so many people have been let down. Already the number of mates I had in the Todd River barely eight years before could now be counted on one hand. I had just buried Kummanjayi Inkamala in November and true to Arrernte custom I had a shaved head.

However, to start university I decided that since I was almost totally outmatched by the task I would go the easiest route to get the runs on the board. I had enrolled in South East Asia studies and political science and politics. I was also studying economics. The major problems were both in and out of my studies. For a start I had no computer literacy, a limited understanding of how to research (though I was still good at it on the level I was!) and I was still mourning over Kumanjayi.

Another task that confronted me was how to diffuse the possibility of what's known as payback in Aboriginal custom. The payback involved was to take Kummanjayi's Balanda or "white" boyfriend to task for her death. This was expected but there were several problems in the way of it being carried out. First, as a Christian with a firm eye on a 100 per cent departure from the way things were done previously, would Jesus do payback? Secondly, the situation, though quiet and though Kumantjayi's (Kummanjai Inkamala's boyfriend of 1985) people and I had shaken hands and resolved our differences, the possibility of payback could potentially put that at risk. The need to keep the peace overshadowed all my decisions when it came to my Indigenous friends. OK, I reasoned God had given me back Darwin, so would He appreciate it if I'd wrecked my only chance? What would I do if I'd given a bloke such a chance and he blew it in such a stupid fashion?

My second highest priority would be to diffuse that

situation, especially as rumours had begun to circulate that my presence in Darwin had more to do with payback rather than an earnest wish to start anew. Therefore, I tracked her boyfriend down and found him sitting in the Smith Street Mall at the taxi rank end of it. At first he looked at me expecting trouble, however I said to him, 'If I claim to be a Christian yet resort to payback then I am not much of a Christian. Also, once it starts it never stops, just becomes a burning fire like those underground coal fires that burn forever, long after what ignited them is forgotten.' With that we shook hands, and made sure every "long grasser" there could see it regardless of who they were. True peace at last! Another one who became a friend.

With the situation now fully resolved, it was time to turn to my other priorities; my university studies and to find a church to attend, something I did not have since recommitting myself to Christ eight months prior. Of course, a quick look at the dreaded Potters House was a sure start. I attended once only and was told in no uncertain terms that I was unwelcome there. The warning was made on the strength of information provided to them by a person who attended there. The information was lies and the man was later exposed as a liar by an Indigenous group he said he was part of. My reply was that I was going to serve God in one way or another regardless of what they said. I rode off back to Parap and stopped on the way home to pick the five corner fruits, coconuts and other local niceties that hung over people's fences that formed my staple diet with the rice and fish that formed my diet when I first returned to Darwin. My bike trailer was full of these things. Just because I was broke did not mean I couldn't eat healthy; a skill I learned in the "Long Grass".

That week a young Indonesian lady studying Psychology told me of her church in Malak on the Northern Suburbs of Darwin. I rode up there, a 13 kilometre one-way ride. I pulled up my bike up against the wall and walked in to what looked like a middle-class church with a few of my Aboriginal friends attending as well. The church was designed on a tropical Darwin open plan. Its walls had the cement blocks laid in such a way that the holes provided ventilation.

There was a very large bloke in front of the congregation and I was very relieved to find out it was the pastor of the church. I thought that I'd found a decent church, but even though I liked the pastor, his vision and the fact that his eldership stuck up for me, I don't think the majority of his flock were quite ready for a rough-looking bloke like me to come along. My church reception was not that good in some ways and even now I can't see why one ex-"Long Grasser" would be so much trouble for them because he definitely just wanted somewhere to worship Christ and make friends.

There were quite a few things that shaped my relationship with the church; some positive some negative. My view was that the church definitely had a vision to reach out to the community that surrounded it and in many ways it reflected the racial makeup of Darwin with 75 out of the 100 or so ethnic groups represented in Darwin represented in the church. It had an Aboriginal outreach in Bagot and other places near and far and to me it was making an effort to reach its community in both a practical and spiritual way that few Pentecostal churches have done.

However, the church was still very much a product of the culture it was in as far as its programmes went and what its unofficial policies seemed to be. For instance, anyone going on the "dole" or other welfare was looked down upon no matter what they did to get work and no matter what they did to better their situation.

I firmly believe that the only strategy to have if you are on the dole is to plan to get off it. However, there are circumstances that force people to remain on welfare and they have to work within the parameters that they find themselves in until they can break free of them. I have the highest respect for a lot of single parents and people on disabilities who really struggle and in some cases their names become household words for all the right and honourable reasons.

In my case and a few others, the fact that I was an ex-"Long Grasser" rather than a person who was attempting to get his life together seemed to be embedded in a lot of heads. Firstly, if I asked for help, quite a few would only begrudgingly do so and they were in the minority. However, it made me resolve to be as self-sufficient as possible and only ask for help if I really needed it.

There were also the hygiene reminders, but never mind that I was by now quite presentable. That stopped when I threatened to floor the bloke who, in loving terms, reminded me of my need to clean up. All these things I did anyway; I worked around the church and in others places voluntarily, and I'd already had a reasonable start on the prejudices of some of the congregation. Therefore, I decided that very little was for free and if I ate at a person's house I'd wash the dishes and if I'd stayed there, a couple of twenty dollar notes would be hidden somewhere, or I'd mow the lawn. This was what I'd done anyway wherever I was and is still my firm policy even when I was in the "Grass" and therefore the anti-freeloading message I found insulting.

A church should be helping people to achieve the goals it sets as should any decent person who has to lay down the law.

Sometimes a bit of hard love is required for the lazy person, whose behaviour reflects badly on the vast majority of the poor and disabled etcetera, and they should be confronted in no uncertain terms. However, to lay down the law as it were to the rest requires tact, love and above all there must always be a credible offer or remedy to give them. If, for example, you have a person with a big business and all they do is talk down but don't lift a finger to help someone get a job then they are an annoying clanging drum! OK, does the Bible agree with the above thoughts? Let's see..

The ominous verse that's trotted out is this one: 2 Thessalonians 3:10, "For even when we were with you, this we commanded you: that if any would not work, neither should he eat." Note, "wouldn't work" means one has the capacity to work and is just lazy!

The need to look after people who are disadvantaged is summed up here: 1 Thessalonians 5:14, "We urge you, brothers and sisters, warn those who are idle and disruptive, encourage the disheartened, help the weak, be patient with everyone."

And Galatians 2:10, "All they asked was that we should continue to remember the poor, the very thing I had been eager to do all along."

Even Ancient Israel had a social security system as they had rules as to what to leave for the poor. They had a "Tithe" which was the payment of a tenth of one's income which was to maintain the temple and act as a poor chest. I really wonder what would happen if a lot of big churches actually used the tithe they were paid in a manner that fits the original purpose of it.

Leviticus 27:30 says, "A tithe of everything from the land, whether grain from the soil or fruit from the trees, belongs to the LORD; it is holy to the LORD." And Leviticus 23:22 states, "When you reap the harvest of your land, do not reap to the very edges of your field or gather the gleanings of your harvest. Leave them for the poor and for the foreigner residing among you. I am the LORD your God."

However, those who say but choose not to assist are like the people who Jesus condemned in the following Scripture. Luke 11:46; "Jesus replied, 'And you experts in the law, woe to you, because you load people down with burdens they can hardly carry, and you yourselves will not lift one finger to help them.'" Again, no wonder the readers of this book are often driven away from the church because a lot of churches are not even thinking like they should.

Therefore, I have a firm attitude of gratitude that I am a citizen of a country that won't let you starve if, for some reason, you can't get a job. Australia, New Zealand and to a much lesser extent Fiji and the French territories and Brunei are the only countries with a social security system in our region! When I was in Fiji there were many beggars and on Bougainville you had men with lawn mowers asking in Tok Pisin (PNG Pidgin), *"Mipela Laikim Wok"* or "I want work". Australians are blessed that they don't have to do that to simply survive.

There I was, an ex-"Long Grasser" trying his hand at University where some of the better police and others in Alice said I belonged, rather than where I was, on Austudy, having to pray through this alien environment inch by inch. Add to this another happening; my parents suddenly divorced. Even though I had not really been with them for a long time, the fact that they were married longer than quite a lot of their friends continuously made me quite proud of them.

My university progress was almost a complete failure in

1992, then steady for the next year and the year after that. In 1992 I got a small motorbike and a driver's licence. In 1994 I had my first accident where a drunken driver ran me down. I was fortunate that I had no major injuries other than one of the bones in my arm that needed a plate. Again, miracle number seven. I was alive and able to work and study despite being hit by the car and the damage to my postie bike was superficial and nothing that could not be fixed with a spanner and a few panelling tools!

The church I attended was also changing; some said for the better and some said definitely for the worse. A "revival" had started in Darwin in late 1992 after an evangelist came up to Darwin bringing a new move from a place called Toronto in Canada. It was very strange. As a veteran of many a drunken party, I saw the church go like that when people were prayed over by the evangelists and leaders. Controlled pandemonium. The fact that the church in general up to that time was following a decent course then suddenly throwing out that course to follow something totally new was very strange to me. However, it soon became obvious that with this new move the place began to decline morally and spiritually. The Bible says, "Test all things, hold on to what is good" (1 Thessalonians 5:11), that is, use the brain God gave you to use! Be people, not sheeple!

After the accident I got a compensation payout and this was soon turned into a DT 175 Yamaha motorcycle. I fitted it with a cargo box and put a chevron on the back of the box and a red/white/blue design on the front in reflector tape.

Myself and what's known as "scotchlite" road sign reflector tape have a very long relationship. I designed the pattern on the bike because if my lights failed the other road users could still see the bike until I managed to get off the road. It would also identify my location in the event of an accident in a remote area. I still have that on my Hilux and trailer to this day.

With everything looking definitely upward, there was one thing left to complete everything. There was something missing from my life, a lady friend! When I initially came to the church there was a young lady studying nursing at the university I attended that I was interested in. She wasn't interested in me though and I still thank God that she wasn't foolish enough to accept my proposal. However, as time went on it seemed as if I would not be finding Mrs Right at the church. A friend of mine from Vanuatu had been studying at the university and had met a lady and after a brief courtship they got married. She had family in Fiji but was purportedly from the Torres Strait. What started alarm bells ringing about her was that I knew people up there and had a bit of knowledge about the Torres Strait, especially Horn Island. When I asked her about it, she couldn't effectively answer my questions.

What she did have was strong links with Fiji. She introduced me to a lady in Fiji named Rakshana Khan, a Muslim girl about 18 years old. I started writing to her at the rate of one letter a week. This discarded a long standing policy of no mail-order-type relationships. As I was lonely and wanting company, and couldn't seem to socialise well in the church, even a bitter spring looked sweet.

There was also the fact that I was after three years of stability and good neighbours, having a major problem with my downstairs neighbour who was mentally ill and screaming all night. I applied for a transfer through the Housing Commission and my behaviour in Alice Springs with them came back to haunt me. The manager at the time was the same one that was in Alice Springs who had transferred north. She was not really wanting to assist me here either. Therefore, after a long struggle I cleared the flat and surrendered the keys moving into the Church Discipleship house on Trower Road.

I used part of my payout to get a ticket to Fiji to see Rukshana and her family. I did this against wise advice of my pastors and friends as the situation with the lady who introduced us was far from certain as well. I arrived in Brisbane and my brother Ian came and took me to my dad's place. I was there for two days and he was called out on a job at the prison (he worked for Q Build as an electrician). I was woken up at five am by Ian who told me that Dad had died from a heart attack (he was age 62). His departing words to me, the last family member to see him alive, was that he was coming back in the morning. My mother came up and Drew did as well and the last photo of us brothers and mum together was taken at this time.

It was decided that Dad would be cremated and since he died intestate the estate would be administered by Drew, and split equally. Ian got the house in Beenleigh. I went to Fiji a few days after and was met at the airport by Rukshana and her family. We only lasted two weeks, as the sister-in-law undermined the relationship and I soon ended up back in Brisbane.

There was a young lady who was in an arranged marriage to one of her brothers. For three years afterwards she begged me to do something to get her out of her situation. Often you can't do something when someone you know is in a bad marriage or relationship and you can only wring your hands and pray. There's a song called *Women in Chains* by Tears for Fears which sums up many a sorry marriage like that one.

While everything with Rukshana was going irrevocably pear-shaped, I met another young lady Ranadi; always a joker with a very nice smile. We became fast friends and my travels took me up to Vaileka and Ba and other places that feature so large in my life today.

I returned to Brisbane and went by bus to Melbourne to see Mum and Drew, then went north to Adelaide and back to Darwin. I still had not written off Rukshana yet and the door was open to her. I think she wanted the relationship but her family shut it down. The matters that were coming to light and into focus were the major un-investigated issues regarding the lady who introduced me to her in the first place. Back in Darwin, the cracks in Lynette Aniba aka "Auntie Jabbien" aka "Aniba aka Mehrul aka Obed"'s story was by now obvious to everyone. She and my friend shifted three times in Darwin in the space of a year, and finally they both left Darwin very suddenly.

As for my poor friend, it appeared as if his wife was using the Aniba name from a family in the Torres Strait again; some of the family were old schoolies of mine. The real Lynette began to get demand letters from Telstra etc that she knew nothing of. The lady impersonating Mrs Aniba even managed to convince the AOG paper "Evangel" to do an article on her when she was in Adelaide. Again, the fact that she said she was studying gynaecology should have made her easy to follow up but enquiries in March lead nowhere.

When I was in the Royal Adelaide Hospital I attempted to find a Lynette Aniba but couldn't. Both her and her poor husband had vanished into thin air; her innocent victim husband was now beginning to see that she was not one but in fact several identities. By the time the Federal police caught up with her, Mehrul Nisha was but one of ten aliases she had and she had three nations' passports, Australian, PNG, and her native Fijian (Nadroga area on the mainland Viti Levu).

The family in Fiji prevented me from following up her story in Fiji; a family there knew everything but was too close to Rukshana's family house for any serious attempt at investigation to be mounted. Add to that my father's passing was very recent and I was unable to bring the effort to bear on resolving the mystery. Information gained in 2002 placed her and my ex-wife together in Sydney.

My letters to Setaita were going out at the rate of one a week and with the university ticking down as best it could, there was every possibility that my target to complete my studies by 1998 would hold. I recommenced University at NTU with eleven units left and was taking management studies as well as two politics units. I resumed staying at the church house in Trower Road. I still rode my motorbike way out of town for prayers and was often quite lonely at times.

Chapter 10

Accident number two

Brachial Plexus Injury or BPI for short; what is it and why am I starting the chapter with it? Well there are nerves in your shoulder that connect from your spine to control your hands and arm. These are known as the Brachial Plexus which is sort of like a distribution box and electrical relay in your car. Brachial Plexus Injury is when the nerve gets torn away; usually it's from motorbike accidents or gunshot wounds to the shoulder. It's a common nerve injury with infants, motorcyclists and horse riders. The injury happens when the arm gets overstretched resulting in the nerve getting torn; in my case, my neck got overstretched when I hit the road.

My story is that I went to a church party and decided to take a long drive down the Stuart Highway out of Darwin to pray. At seven-thirty pm I had just changed to top gear and was sitting on the speed limit about 500 meters past the turnoff to Berrimah Jail when there was a huge hit to the back of my motorcycle, propelling me head first into the Stuart highway. I blacked out and my memory is still a bit vague as to what happened, but I remembered that I was soon in an ambulance and was severely injured but didn't know just how severely. My own accident rehearsal kicked in and I was repeating the church contact number as well as that of the discipleship house and a friend that soon had Peter Van Roden and someone else from the church up at the hospital. I was doped up and according to them "I was black and blue from head to foot". I didn't know it but my right lower leg had been crushed because the gearshift had gone straight through it, my neck had been broken or fractured, and I had nerve injury that felt like boiling water was being poured down my arm.

My first week in hospital was like the next ten, totally bed-ridden with a steel frame holding my leg together. Somehow I adjusted OK and managed to shift my handwriting from my right to my left hand; back to where it was at Exmouth in fact. Another friend Rob Jenkins had taken a picture of my motorbike. Apparently the police told him it was the worst non-fatality as far as damage to the bike was concerned; the back wheel had been stored in and the attempted hit and run was foiled by the fact that the bike was wedged on to the front of the vehicle that hit me. The drunk driver blew 0.271.

At the time I assumed that I could rescue my life and things would return to normal after a few months. My contingency plan was based on that premise. University was suspended but only for that semester and I decided to keep things "ready to go" as I was convinced that my time in hospital would only be six months or so at the most. When I withdrew from the semester I did get a whopping great bill from Austudy — the agency that paid the student allowance here in Australia — for 790 dollars soon after my admission. I was soon on the TIO motor accidents benefits which were substantially more than I was getting on Austudy but I lost my low income status which would work against me in the long term.

I continued to pay rent to the house as I thought the accident had effectively put my residence there on hold and I could build up a credit for when I came out. Though I put up with the food, I wasn't going to do that for long. I needed something better. The problem was I had no mobile phone; I had to get someone else to use my key card to get cash, and to buy pizza I had to get someone to call in as ordering was not permitted on the ward phone. At first the visitors from the church came steady but as they saw the stay was long-term the visits dropped off and only three people kept up the effort as well as Scott Lamshed's Bible study. When I got out of bed I attended every week in July or August but I'm still unsure as to when I was able to move around.

Again the situation at the church was duplicated at this study and the fact that the "manifestations" were required ALL the time meant that there were deep nagging questions as to whether or not this was actually of God. I was in severe pain with the Brachial Plexus Injury all the time and really started to wonder if God was really doing anything at times. One day blurred into another and several times I actually lost track of day, date and time.

Of course, there were miracles already; I was not a quadriplegic for a start and the major transitions with things such as my handwriting went smoothly. I was getting rehabilitation, but the pain that came with this injury meant I was always extremely uncomfortable and in an often contorted position, even in public. What would often overload others was not overloading me because of the thought that Jesus heals things like this and Philippians 4:17 says "I can do all things through Christ who strengthens me".

The starting point was not going to be my hospital time but when the doctors gave me a chilling assessment of where I was at that time. The doctor's verdict was clear; there were ten things that I would never do again. They were:

1. Ride a bicycle.

2. Heavy work.

3. Welding and such skills.

4. Drive any motor vehicle.

5. Resume university above a part-time load.

6. Walk more than 600 meters unaided.

7. Be able to organise and manage complex functions.

8. Use my right arm beyond the limp hanging-down way it was.

9. Weight bear on my right leg.

10. Walk without a stick.

All up, not much from then on.

A potentially devastating king hit. One gets news from a doctor like that but doesn't get up most times. However, I had a lot of times where I felt Jesus had delivered me and worked miracles, therefore like in a court of law, my prayers to Jesus were being framed in what he had done before. In law, this is known as the Doctrine of Precedence and this means that a case before a judge is argued from legislation but also in the light of cases before it that had rendered a decision close to what's being argued. That's what is used when you mount a case and one can build a strategy to plan but also to pray. My physical strategy followed my spiritual one.

My aim was to get back on my feet as much as possible

and my plan was already developing by the time this assessment arrived. Therefore, the assessment and the accident began to seem like a challenge to me, like Goliath was to Israel, a blatant insult levelled by the devil at the very Jesus I claimed to serve as Lord and His promises! I went out in my wheelchair and said to Jesus as Jehovah the healer, "OK I have their opinion, what's yours?" It was me challenging Jesus for his opinion of what was said and a demand for an answer for what he would do to fix it. You see, too many people think that you have to be a bit afraid of God. Me, I think He is a Big God who isn't afraid of a direct challenge as to what He thinks of one's situation.

Of course, there is no room for a cavalier attitude when it comes to doctors and their recommendations. The staff at Royal Darwin Hospital were very professional and anyone who thinks faith is a licence to disregard doctors' advice and stop taking medications you are on, I say to them in no uncertain terms to wake up. God puts those who are in the medical field there to help you and advise you. Don't be a fool and disregard their words and don't listen to anyone who advises you to do the same. That's called "Spiritual abuse" and is rampant in many, though not all, churches. Miracles are called miracles because they are... well.. miracles.

Of course, I've had my share of them. Since the accident I've survived cancer, multiple attempts at killing myself (that's what accidents etc. are, especially when they cause injury), people have threatened to "line me up" with a motor car while I'm riding by bicycle in the desert, they have threatened me with spearing and a bullet. I've had that many close calls that I've lost count; things like my recent cancer scare where I was in hospital for two months.

I have also managed to improvise and make use of my

disabilities in such a way that I can do most things myself. That in itself is a miracle of God. However, we are all a work in progress and are all precious in His sight no matter what the world's voices may say. There is going to be a book on Brachial Plexus Injury in the near future with the way I have managed to adapt and work with it.

I regarded the accident, and the report that came after it, as an insulting challenge to my God, the Lord God of Israel, an affront to everything I hold dear in a very obscene fashion. As such, they need to be challenged in prayer and challenged in the Lord. The above needed to be resisted and overcome as much as possible from word go. I had a good legal ally on this too, as the Motor Accident Compensation Act in the NT obligated the victim to get as much pre-accident function back as possible. Therefore, my strategy would be just that. Ranadi said she would hang on as we both thought that I'd be out of hospital and on the mend by November at the latest. However, I regarded the Fiji solution as more of a default position rather than a firm plan. See how Ranadi and I turned out, give her chances to say no, and I could rethink the plan I had. All she needed to do was to say "No" and the whole mess that happened would never have happened!

Also there was an Aboriginal lady, Kumanjayi Cooke from Lajamanu, who was a good friend for years and that looked like it might be a long-term commitment. However, the case against my asking her out was the fact that my history saw my relationships with ladies like Kumanjayi going south or ended up in other problems would put a lot of reasons for me not being more serious with her. My history played against what might have been a decision that might have saved a lot of heartache and loss.

She had another friend of mine Kumanjayi Knight as her

boyfriend. I decided it was wise to simply respect that as it stood. Not only had I needed to keep things in the church reasonable, but also the wider picture for me was that I didn't want to have a rerun of having to leave Darwin in the middle of the night again because Mr Knight's extended family might have got involved in our conflict and this time a much larger area of the NT would potentially be a no-go area for me. It could have also ended any time in the NT. Therefore, I decided to keep the peace. For that and other reasons meant it never progressed beyond a friendship.

Let what happened in 1985 stay there. My relationship with the local Aboriginal people was very good and anything that rocked that particular boat would have to be either carefully done or not done at all. However, she was a lifeline to me at a critical time when most things were down and out. I wrote the manuscript to "Southern Star" in 1996 for the third time since 1979. This is a still as yet unpublished novel about an invasion of Australia and PNG by an Indonesian led confederacy. The manuscript was approved for publication but resources have stalled the project.

In November, my leg was a non-union fracture and they decided to send me to Royal Adelaide Hospital for a nerve transplant. I then had to add another three months at least to my stay which started to strain things a bit with Ranadi in Fiji. By now I was in communication with her people in Rakiraki as well as with her and her family in Ba.

The church still had the Toronto/Darwin thing going and I was by now getting increasingly cynical of it. Several people said God was calling me to account for things I said in the NT News etc. Financially I was the best off I'd been in years but there were deep cracks in my relationship with the church I was attending and the more I saw of this new path the church was taking and its fruit the wider those cracks became. I simply put on a face for now as I looked for an exit point where I could keep the good people I'd met but get out of the runaway train's path.

My loyalty was to Jesus first. I was having thoughts of getting out of the church but dismissed them. The reason was that my brain had built a cage around me. I couldn't think the way I wanted others to think about me, that what God was building is what should be focussed upon. I had 27,000 dollars and could rent anywhere in Darwin. However, due to my own past of poverty, the poverty mentality kept me tied to a post and not really investigating other options.

I kept track of the days, 30 grew to 200 then on and on. December 1996 was spent in hospital as was the first three months of 1997. My leg twice refused to heal and my nerve injury had major surgery done on it. My right arm hung limp and I was stuck in a wheelchair but I wanted to go to Fiji to Ranadi. God was in fact preventing me going but I was oblivious to this. I was released from hospital in April 1997 and went to stay at an Aboriginal hostel for three weeks where I actually began to walk on my own!

I went back to the church accommodation on Trower road, bought a pushbike and had an accident breaking my leg again. My plan to go to Fiji was in ruins again. With Ranadi, it was the straw that broke the camel's back. However, being confined to the house was a good and bad thing; good because it gave me a closer relationship with the Lord, and bad because I saw two youth group members' relationship get a lot more intimate than it should have been. I had a choice; do I tell the eldership in the knowledge that it could well be pushed under the rug, or do I keep quiet? I chose the latter and the man the girl was with went on to cause a lot of damage in other young ladies' lives. However, I still believe that this "new path" they were following made them quite blind as to what was really happening in their midst.

To end this chapter, the fact that I have survived not one but two drink-driving accidents makes for my very firm belief that those who choose to drink and get drunk then choose to get behind the wheel deserve the same treatment as if they chose to do that with a firearm. My Hilux weighs about 2100 kilos without the trailer so that is 2100 kilos of steel flying along at 100km/hr at times. Put some innocent person in front of it and a drunk at the wheel and it's a weapon; the same penalties for misuse of a firearm should be applied to misuse of cars by drunken drivers.

Though the Lord has healed quite a lot of the injuries to the extent that I can function well, I am still affected by the accident to this day. I am hoping to write another book on the subject of BPI so that people who are like me can be encouraged and I can show them what I can do thanks to Jesus my Lord.

Chapter 11

Ni Sa Bula Nia Viti... (Welcome to Fiji)

I left Darwin on the tenth of October 1997 and was met at Nadi by Ranadi and her family. We went up to the house in Ba and stayed there a few days. I noted that all wasn't the way it should be with Ranadi and couldn't put my figure on it. Regardless, we went up to Rakiraki and the village of Waimari to stay with Ranadi's family there, which was headed by a matriarch named Miliana. I called her Bubu or "Grandmother". She was very dignified, a bit humorous at times but her whole being screamed a great mature relationship with the Lord, the type of pillar that holds it all together. The accommodation was a room which they vacated for Ranadi and I in the tin house which was devoid of electricity. All up a nice setting under the Nakauvadra Ranges which formed the south and east boundary of our valley. There was an Assemblies of God in the village of Vatusekiyasawa which I attended.

Generally, people were good and very helpful, but not all. For a start, if I took a taxi anywhere I had to double check the fare with a friend before I paid up or the taxi would overcharge, and ditto to everything else if you were not really careful.

The village's Assemblies of God church was pastored by a husband and wife team. He was local and she was from Batiki in the Lomaiviti Islands and they had four kids. I'd go to church and come back in the night to the "house on the hill" as I'd call it after staying the day at the pastor's house. It seems as if I was in just the right place as my rehabilitation was now forced rather than optional. First my injuries had me take taxis everywhere and at five dollars one way to town (that's when they were not overcharging) it was expensive, the healing was starting, and I was soon walking in breaks the two kilometers to church. That was one area where God was healing. Unfortunately for my young wife having an injured white fella hanging off her must have been a bit shame-faced.

Ranadi and I got married on the 22nd of October 1997. The stepfather said that we married without his consent when in fact he did give me his consent in a letter a few months earlier. Ranadi and I went to Tovata in Suva and I attempted to enrol in USP there in order to attempt to finish my disrupted university studies. The charges were very high and required up front, so that put an end to that idea. We came back to Rakiraki. I presented a sevusevu (traditional offering) to the chief in Tovata for some land but lost the photos. Ranadi and my relationship was tense and I hoped my heart would be of more appeal to Ranadi and lift her spirits.

There was more stuff lurking like land mines under the ground; things that would shame the whole family, innocent and guilty alike. These issues helped me think of ways of not repeating the experiences for anyone else, they made me a lot more forthright about things in my life. What motivated the stepfather to act was summed up thus; the fact was that I was sending a few dollars to Ranadi when I was in Darwin and the stepfather was getting the money. No Ranadi or Keith = no money. A week before Christmas a pastor at another AOG Church in Rakiraki told me that the stepfather was going to attempt to abort the marriage and take Ranadi back to extort cash. I think, though I am not definite.

He had blessed the marriage in the Fijian way and they held a ceremony which the family went to great effort to hold. My contribution to the disaster was that rather than stay alert and watch out, I didn't. He took action and on the 27th of December he provoked an argument and took Ranadi back to Ba. A month later the whole mess exploded when Ranadi gave birth prematurely. I went with some of the family down to Ba to see Ranadi on the twenty-seventh of January 1998. I can still remember the grandmother's words to the stepfather, in Fijian but translated here: 'You bought this man to Fiji from Australia for this and this disgrace happened. You are rubbish, rubbish!' The result was a huge rupture in the family which was to spread out to touch a few others as well. Me, I felt betrayed yes, but the whole lot of them were not responsible, only a few that one could count on one hand and the shame this bought them affected me also. I decided that in spite of the fact that the little one was not mine that it was not his fault and I'd simply take him on. He died on the 13th of January, three days of life. I was back in Ra when that happened.

I didn't hold anyone accountable but definitely wanted to know who the father of that little one was. At first I accused the wrong man then the answer came a long time later as did the reason the "coup" happened. Add to that the real father of Ranadi was the AOG Pastor in the village. Since it was hidden from his wife it nearly tore the family apart. However, my deepest sympathy was and still is for Ranadi who, as far as I was concerned, was pushed into something she didn't want in the first place. To her credit she attempted to keep the marriage going for the brief two months; it lasted until our divorce on the 10th of August 1998 and was rubber stamped by me out of sympathy upon my return to Fiji. It's funny that August 10th is when I mark my anniversary of leaving home in 1983, though I left home in December.

However, amidst all this mayhem a miracle happened. I was sleeping one evening and dreamt that my right arm could move. I woke up and it was moving for the first time since the accident, 15th of February 1998. I took a photo of it and the whole family was praising God that my arm could move at the elbow at last!

About the same time news was leaking out from Darwin that all was not well at the church back in Darwin; the true fall out was beginning in the church. It was falling in numbers and importance. I often say that if I'd stayed in Darwin at the church it would be very unlikely this would be written as I possibly would, like so many others, have walked off. However, my stand was the same as with the Potters House, whatever may come I will serve Jesus with or without them. The result was quite a few people I knew then have walked away from Christ because of what happened in the church when this laughing revival hit. They took their eyes off the prize and lost their way.

"By their fruits you will know them" (Matthew 7:16, 20). From where I am standing, the fruit of that movement was the sheer damage it left behind and the fact that even though it spread across the Pentecostal movement it's not mentioned that much today in good company it seems. Everything this thing touched ended up hurt in some way. I have been around Australia and seen church after church either disbanded or extinct everywhere this movement touched.

Three months later I returned to Fiji intending this time to stay for good. I resumed living in Rakiraki at Vatusekiyasawa village with the AOG pastor's family there. Several things I noted about Fijian's perceptions of Australia, were that Australia consisted of Sydney, Melbourne, and possibly Brisbane and nothing else, and that it was always cold and there were money trees growing everywhere. Of course, to tell someone in the village that 380 Australian dollars a week would barely pay your rent in Australia was just not possible. To tell them that in your part of the world it was hotter and grew many of the same things as Fiji was unbelieved. Even these days I have many of them who think that Darwin's a suburb of Sydney and Kununurra is a four hour or so drive from Darwin. The income in the village is about F$60 a week on a good market week or F$15 a day if you are cutting cane, so telling someone that five times the sixty would barely pay the rent in Australia is just mindboggling to them.

Generally, things settled down in Vatusekiyasawa and the differences with Ranadi's family resolved after we divorced in August 1998. I had resolved however, to put the power on at her relative's place as a sign of goodwill and respect for the grandmother who oversaw the clan up there. There were decent developments happening and I got residency and was already talking to the pastor regarding a place to stay as I was under his cramped roof and wanted them to regain the room I was in. He gave me a piece of land to build on.

I didn't want to be seen as a freeloader and also that as a member of the village I had to obey its rules and contribute if I could. I made a fair old mess of some etiquette and other things one did and didn't do in the village as I fumbled my way in this voyage of discovery. How the touraga Ni koro (Head Man) didn't call me in was a miracle!

For example, on Diwali night in 1998 I got about twelve large firework rockets and set them off so they went off overhead of the village. This was a definite no-no but I didn't get into any trouble over it! Instead the howls of both delight and frustration in the village could be heard from our place which was 400 yards from the village.

A development strategy that fitted my own limited finances was put together and soon lights were on in houses that had no electricity. The solution was two multi-plug power boards, a tube light and extension cord running from one house to another; it would change lives. My thinking was and still is on force multipliers rather than big expensive ventures that are not flexible. Often these schemes are problems themselves being made to fit a solution from a Western eye rather than the local situation. Whether in Indigenous Australia or overseas I really wonder how much money might have been saved if those with it would listen to the advice of those at a grass roots level. Electricity is the greatest force multiplier and for 70 Fijian dollars, one could with the help of a neighbour put a thatched bure (house) on power rather than dangerous and polluting kerosene lanterns. The second thing was that the women and kids were sliding around like cattle on the greasy paths around the village. "Vaka nai bullumakau," as one grandmother told me. Two tonne of cement plus a few blokes equals a roughly one to two kilometre footpath network that was built upon over the years.

I had bought land in Lautoka and was planning the construction of a house on it and was involved in assisting the villagers at Natokita to get power on by December 1998. I even began to date a girl from the village by then and Ranadi's family were on reasonable terms with me so everything was looking good in my new home. I thought I'd found happiness at last. I had even bought tin to start building a house in the land the pastor said I could build on.

Chapter 12

When things go pear shaped; Fiji 1999-2000

Christmas of 1998 would be remembered for me as getting a girlfriend who seemed to be on the ball. The lady who walked into my life at first was very nice and I hoped at last something was about to happen that was beneficial to my long-term welfare and hers. She was the sister of the pastor's wife and had been in Australia for an unknown amount of time. By her knowledge of Australia I'd say not long, maybe a year if that and she had a child there, Nelson, who was looked after by the pastor in Ba. We got on well and fast fell into a relationship by Christmas. My plan was to marry, but for us to remain in Ra until I could get the house in Lautoka finished. The day after we married the situation looked more like a hostile takeover than a real marriage. It began to pan out that her plan and motives were way different to my own.

We married on the 5th of January 1999 in Ba. A few days after I married Watiqu we were on the receiving end of a letter that was written by Ranadi. It was what her stepfather told her just before he took her back to Ba on the 27th of December 1997. It was the reason she so willingly returned to her father that day. It had in it many allegations against me which in Aboriginal custom would have resulted in my death long before I hit Fiji. It was to be fourteen years before it would finally be dealt with. In the end Ranadi owned up and apologised. It would rank as the worst and most damaging set of accusations levelled against me because it was ruinously successful in two countries. "The gospel according to Ranadi" I called it and it was my very own version of "Protocols of the Elders of Zion" i.e. something that was put together to slander and destroy and then believed by a large group of people. Watiqu spread it far and wide and was seemed as if those who heard it had believed it, so defending myself against the accusations was a complete waste of time. Eventually, Ranadi apologised and we are good friends now as we all confessed our many sins to each other.

The marriage, as I said, looked like a hijack and I was being diverted to an unknown place. I had the responsibility of two kids thrust upon me. The situation was fragile. I asked the pastor in Ba to keep Nelson until we were stable enough. The boy, Nelson, was in far better hands than ours and would go far if that status quo remained. However, that was not to happen. So I inherited Gloria who didn't like me at the time and a five-year-old girl. And Nelson who was eleven and needed the stability and home life we definitely could not provide.

I was out of my depth in many ways. What emerged was a total travesty to the concept of a home I had. In Nelson's case a simple decision to house him with us against my express wishes left a boy who was top of his class at primary school end up as a drug-dependent young man supporting his habit by theft and eventually he ended up in jail as an adult. I just hope the Nelson I knew there gets back to where he should be and we can reconcile and help each other. Any other outcome is just not acceptable for anyone calling himself a son of the highest. Nelson has begun to get his life in order at last with the help of the family in Fiji and that state of affairs seems to be holding.

Chapter 12

Firstly, I was facing the full force of something I was utterly not equipped for. Spiritually there were a lot of things happening that left me almost completely unable to effectively regain control over my life, my finances, and so forth. For a start, Watiqu used to boast about her Chiefly Heritage all the time and used to justify everything she did as from God. She would be very boastful and showy about the new wealth she suddenly had compared to her family. The more time went by the more strained the relationship. In February I attempted to flee but she came and took me back; this was a waste of time. She could convince everyone of her point of view which resulted in, 'They have already made their mind up so why bother?' Any attempt at redressing what was a very twisted path was met with repeated slogans and abuse.

In short, a complete affront to everything I stood for and the Fijian traditions and customs I love and uphold. A chief is a humble person who serves his subjects and is thankful for those who support him in his office. He doesn't boast about himself or herself. A good pastor, preacher, or prophet does not hold their badge of office up boastfully. At least a real one doesn't. Contrary to what many believe, there are great and honest people out there who are filling these three great offices of the church, and I'm glad to say they are in the majority.

My idea of a house is way different to many other people. To me the villagers had houses and homes, the pastor in Vatusekiyasawa had a home and a house, regardless of its leaky roof and outside toilet etc. like everyone else. But for me who has lived worse before knew it and others were actually homes; yes tin, yes wood, yes devoid of power in most cases, simply furnished but homes they were.

We had rented a three-bedroom house on Kings Road

which was soon filled with furniture and other items. 'This isn't my house, it's just a sleeping place,' I said to Watiqu, as me like her father, were simple men liking simple things. Her father Samisoni was a very wise old man who seemed to have a voice in high places. A simple army trained man who loved kids, a talanoa (Fijian talk sessions that can go far into the night, I used to call it sleep saving) and we both loved politics. This could really rile Watiqu who was pregnant with Kathleen at the time. Money was flowing out in a bid to keep up appearances and I'd lost control. In short Watiqu ran the show. The contrast between her and the family was stark.

Often anything that was said ended up with a visit from the pastor or others. In short physically, spiritually and mentally I was in free fall. In July my prayers were answered with things starting to bottom out, as it seemed that God was still listening to my cries. However, they did not improve the way Watiqu wanted them to. Things with Watiqu and the church deteriorated as Watiqu would tell them what was going on and members would attempt to pressure me into this and that. One day I said to one member, 'My deliverer is standing by, he's watching and waiting his time.' Soon I changed churches to another one in another place. Relations with Watiqu soured over this as loyalty to church often is on the same level as loyalty to the family in Fiji. 'You go to church where the family tells you, not where you want to," my former brother-in-law in Sydney remarked. We never got on which I think is a tragedy considering that his wife and family were and still are held in highest regard by me, having prayed and cried with me when things were visibly falling to bits. With things going sour I asked the Lord for His direct intervention. By December I was at the new church and this saw improvement due to a firm and friendly pastoral hand.

Chapter 12

The pastor and his wife were great people, like the ones in the church I'd left to join the new church. However, things were still deteriorating at home fast and a man who couldn't control his wife or family was not a man in the Fijian or even Melanesian tradition so my stocks plummeted in many people's eyes.

In October two things happened. The first was that Kathy was born. We decided to name Kathleen for my mother and one of the strongest ladies in the church Watiqu attended. They were like many old Fijian women, pillars of their community. Her last name before Gregory was Watiqu's mother's name; Adi Fulori.

The second thing was that the money ran out which made things a little tight. The problem was there was way too much going out including a 300 a month phone bill that was reverse charge calls from everywhere in Fiji. I told the callers that I was not an ATM but was not listened to. As a result I smashed the phone by power-slamming it into the floor. "Talaraka nai televoni" (destroy the phone). I put it up on its holder with the inscription written in pental pen; "THIS PHONE DIED FROM TOO MANY REVERSE CALLS".

Christmas was, for the kids, perhaps the most well-endowed as far as gifts were, but was marked by arguments between Watiqu and myself.

In the New Year of 1999/2000 we went to a church service at a village near Ba. I left the meeting early and attempted to walk back to Ba town on a walking stick in the middle of the night. I got disoriented and didn't know that I was actually walking down the centreline of the road. A carrier (utility car) almost collected me. I reckon that once again God thought that silly bloke was worth his effort. I went home and attempted to sleep. The turning point actually came one month after Christmas. I fasted and asked the Lord for his immediate intervention, like a bankrupt going to a receiver who told him repeatedly not to do as he did. After over a month of fasting the Lord began to take action.

In February 2000 the World Festival of Praise was on in Lautoka. Though Watiqu stayed home, I went. It was drizzling the last night of it and my mates were down in the showground in Lautoka. I was hanging about the stairs to the reserved area and suddenly two large blokes in security uniforms carried me up the stairs by surprise. If you look at the footage of the event, I am standing near a bloke waving an Israeli flag and Brian Houston (the head pastor from Hillsong in Sydney) was to my left at the podium.

Again, the Lord Jesus was listening to me and another promotion of sorts with a message seemed to happen. After a week I went to Suva for business and attended a Barry Smith service.

The countdown to my trip over to Sydney was on. The purpose was to attempt to publish what was to become this book. It was not the best draft either. Remember the Skyscraper? That one was built on sand. There were however, a lot of things deteriorating to the point where staying in Fiji was no longer a viable or safe option for me.

I had bought a house in Ba town at Yalalevu and wanted Watiqu and the kids to move over to it. However it required some repairs and a contractor was engaged to do the job. He kept on delaying the project even though I could not reschedule my departure. April came and the house was meant to be ready but wasn't; the contractor dragged his feet to the extent that I confronted him at his temple the week before I left.

On the fifteenth of April I was in town, checking my box at the post office. A cheque for 670 Fiji dollars was in the box.

Chapter 12

This plus the 800-dollar bank cheque formed my total capital to go to Sydney the next day. I had declared to God that the situation had now deteriorated to the point that it wasn't safe at home anymore. I went secretly to Nadi, booked my ticket and came home. Watiqu had been angry for a few days even though I had made commitments to the Social Welfare they would be looked after whilst I was away, which was only supposed to be three months. However, what I faced when I came home was simply not a safe position for me. Watiqu had thrown a bar at me over the road before I went to town that morning. At last, I packed three sets of trousers, three shirts, and the documents, and swiftly made my exit. As we backed out, Watiqu came at me with a steel bar and my last words to her from a taxi driven by a driver frightened out of his wits was; 'If God's telling you to do it, do it.'

We drove to my pastor's house and a funny thing happened; it seemed as if God sent a huge rain storm to cover my getaway which lasted from when I arrived at their house to when I left, exactly to the minute. It covered my "escape", then I went to Nadi and stayed overnight at a cheap hotel.

Sydney; a place they all knew but I didn't. Sydney; the butt of my coarse jokes especially regarding the homosexuals there. Sydney; the city everyone thinks *is* Australia to the resentment of all those peasants like myself who live far away from it. Sydney; where the "Chester Hill Miracle" an ex-RAAF base was bought by the Southern Cross Bible College (and later sold to an Islamic group for three times its purchase price) was to be my next home. I rang SCBC aka the Bridal College because so many who went to it were single when they went in and married when they came out. They confirmed they had rooms available and I had just enough to cover the rent.

However, I didn't know Sydney and had no idea what Watiqu was telling her brother about my departure. I decided I might be staying with them a while too in Waitara in Sydney's northern suburbs and I had no idea what my reception would be. After a night in Nadi I left Fiji for what I thought was six months, but I had no idea that I'd be returning only in 2013/2014 and then in 2015. Those kids I loved would be adults or teenagers. A regret that I have is that I felt as if my rightful place with Kathy and Gloria and Nelson was stolen and that this contributed to the situation Nelson would find himself involved in.

Chapter 13

Healing Time; Sydney 2000

I left Fiji on the morning of the 16th of April 2000 and arrived in Sydney that afternoon. One member of the family offered to put me up and I assured them that it was only for a few days until I got a roadmap and found where the Bible College was. Their flat was two bedrooms and I wanted to be out of their way as soon as possible. Watiqu's brother raised objections though the main tenant of the house didn't mind a few days. But first to get there; bus to Central then train to Waitara. This was all new to me in a city I knew nothing about.

The next day I started my scouting about in Sydney. I found the Southern Cross College Campus and showed them the bank cheque from Fiji. They graciously allowed me to take a room and I put the cheque into the ANZ bank to be processed. There were also some remaining shares I got sold to fund my stay there. That night, feeling quite pleased with my efforts and God's provision, I went back to the unit and assured Watiqu's brother that I had the means to be out of their hair the very next day.

He was very upset with me and an argument ensued in which I decided it was much healthier if I left rather than stick around. Within an hour I was on the train to the city with suitcase and stick in hand. I stayed overnight in the Youth Hostel then booked in and paid some of the rent in the Bible

College. Sydney was a totally new experience for me; it was a huge city that seemed to go on forever. Within a short time, I had a church and was a member of the local Full Gospel Businessmen's Fellowship at Parramatta. I started praying and fasting and seeking God as I fought the problems emanating from Fiji as well as the fact that I couldn't support the mortgage there and the maintenance at the same time.

I asked Watiqu to use the tools etc. that were there and set up a place in the carport for the youth in the church to learn trades in order to start raising money as the money from Australia was not able to last long. In this I was no better or worse than any other father with these obligations. After all, who has not had Mum working for the food and Dad providing the mortgage? She had many good ideas. If she wanted to remain where she was she had to use them fast. I was ignored and blamed for leaving them even though everyone knew I had to leave and in the manner in which I left. I had as my goodbye gesture a threat made to my life not once but twice and my introduction to the family in Sydney got off to a bad start. A month in I was praying and the question of whether or not I was in the right place was always in my mind.

Then the coup in Fiji definitely put an end to my immediate return. The May 19th coup in Fiji had drastic effects on everyone, me included. In any case, the three months of time I had allotted had just gotten impossible to keep at a stroke. The elected government was overthrown by a group of individuals with George Speight as the front man (though not as incorrectly reported in the mass media as the coup leader). To say it mildly, the way Mahendra Chaudhry ran things was too pragmatic for the cultural environment he was in. He wanted to do investigations into some of the more questionable things that had gone on before his party got elected by landslide in 1999. However, simple pragmatism has its limits. In many ways he came across as abrasive and arrogant and lost most of that massive reservoir of goodwill by December 1999.

Another problem was that we expected Tupeni Baba, his deputy, to take the PM's post but Chaudhry took the oath of office before anyone was aware of him doing it. In fact, the late Adi Kuini Speed, a coalition partner to Chaudhry only found out by virtue of the live broadcast on Fiji One just like the rest of us! Samisoni Lele said his days were numbered as did Watiqu and a lot of others. I didn't want to agree with them but saw that if the way Chaudhry came across with the pragmatic way he put things in place he was gone, by vote of no confidence or by coup. The first Indo-Fijian prime minister was to be Fiji's last in short order. Tensions continued to build through 2000 and the atmosphere when I left was tense.

Suddenly we were cut off as unions in Australia and refused to handle Fiji's mail and services. Even telephone was disrupted for a short time. Effectively there was no government in Fiji and the military held only a tenuous hold on the place as there were defectors from their camp who had taken up residence in the parliament where Chaudhry and his cabinet were held at gunpoint and being forced to resign under duress.

Fiji slid towards anarchy in June and only prayer prevented it from actually crossing the line into inter-confederacy civil war. Places I knew were demolished, people I knew were bashed up, robbed, and in several places killed. A place in Tovata in Suva (Kalabu School) became a place where, for a few weeks, Fiji's future tottered whilst those in power and influence abrogated the responsibilities expected of those who lead. Ranadi and I lived a few hundred yards away from that place where Speight was eventually arrested in 1997.

Eventually the army had lured Speight into a trap and arrested him. President Ratu Mara was forced to stand down and a caretaker administration was installed under Laisenia Qarase who remained Prime Minister winning two elections for the Fijian backed SDL until he was overthrown by Bainimarama in 2006. This raises many questions as to what was really going on which is well outside my scope.

My personal position was that I am firmly in favour of the inalienable right of Fiji's Indigenous people to have their customs and land rights uninterrupted by any government. Like everywhere, the culture of the Indigenous Fijians is vulnerable to outside influences that are often destructive to a basic system of order and discipline and definitely need to be protected if Fiji is to continue what is a very unique mission as a nation to this troubled world. However, there are other communities, like the great leader and war hero Ratu Sir Lala Sukuna who set up much of the protective machinery of government that protected Fijian land and rights. He stated, 'Fiji is like a three-legged stool; it needs all communities to stand'. The others, such as the Indians, all have a right to call Fiji home as well.

The coup in 2006 was a product of the 2000 coup. The Coup Leader, Frank Bainimarama, said that it would be the last. Initially we thought an opportunity had arrived to get Fiji to the great place it should be rather than with the coup culture that infected its politics. I used to call it the "Infrastructure Government" as suddenly there was a lot of help from non-traditional sources such as China and Russia as Australia effectively shut down telling Bainimarama to hold election. It was a good example of why so-called Foreign Aid is not giving cash away. It should be rightfully called "Strategic Expenditure" as that's what it is. The reason why

Australia can put offshore processing centres in foreign countries and undermine the sovereignty of them in the way they are run is an example of what comes from this "Aid". At 3000 dollars per million in the budget I can't think of a more powerful government expenditure with such high returns on investment. As China made more loans to Fiji, yes a lot of stuff got done that was way overdue including powerlines, docks, roads built, and a hydro-station expanded. There was also the emergence of a welfare state.

However by the time I returned I was seeing a much darker side to it. Firstly, the government was getting further and further into debt with its Chinese benefactors. Secondly, the 1997 Constitution, the only legal one in the land, one that took many hard years to put together, was torn up and replaced by another ill-consulted document: the 2013 Constitution, which concentrated power, had a bill of rights with clauses with the rights that can be used to nullify them, and a host of other problems. My research was done in Darwin before I went back to Fiji in 2013. The fact that I was totally independent of anyone in Fiji but came up with similar conclusions to the opposition lawyers says something.

To conclude, as a result of the examination of the politics that emerged post-2006, they held an election in Fiji in 2014 under a very confusing though non-racial system that confused even the most intelligent. The power is concentrated in the hands of four people as this book goes to press. The media is muzzled and there has been a conveyor belt type procession of expatriate management that often resigns in short order. There has been an attempted expropriation of foreign-owned land with no just terms applied and in several cases the owners were deported without reason. The land question has been put off by the constitution which says it backs Fijian land ownership but the mechanics of Itaukei (Fijian) land administration has in fact made it easier to alienate Indigenous land via long-term lease than simple expropriation over time. Opposition politicians are often bought before the courts on non-issues to prevent them standing for elections. There was a raid by the Chinese police carried out with scant regards to human rights procedure or constitutional safeguards to a land with the death penalty.

A country I love and people I respect since my childhood is in very uncertain waters indeed. Once again Fiji needs our prayers like never before at the time of writing.

I was only to be in Sydney for three months, but was forced to cancel my return ticket and wait upon the Lord. "When you see the wind blow in the tops of the balsam trees" was the Bible verse that came out when I was praying about future progress (2 Sam 5:24). Well, balsam was a healing thing to my knowledge and I was still on a walking stick and had running sores down my leg from the steel in it. Basically I was in Sydney until that was taken care of.

The doctor that reviewed my medical requirements was a Palestinian Arab who had fled in 1948, called himself a Christian, but mouthed off as anything but. However, he and I got on fine in spite of my love for Israel; a lot of hands flying around but a handshake at the end of it all. Same as the local Lebanese. I was grateful for the hospitality and friendship the Lebanese I dealt with showed me. Yes, they listened as I had recounted the miracle my life was up to at that point.

The "Chester Hill Miracle" (AKA SCBC) needed to make some cash and it was decided to close it down over the Olympics and lease it out to SOCOG for the Olympics which meant everybody had to relocate. This caused some problems with me as I was in hospital with nowhere to go. I eventually ended up in Woolloomooloo overnight, then at the AOG church in Lakemba, then at a bloke's place in Bankstown. I was happy to have a roof over my head but exhausted by the things that were happening in Fiji both with the country and with my marriage.

The Olympics was on that year and my stay in hospital coincided with the opening ceremony. Auburn Hospital had a bird's eye view of it from a distance. However, one thing that hit me was the massive cuts the NSW Government seemed to have made to stage this thing. For a start the hospital I was in had the middle floors closed. The steel was removed from my leg and the results were fast to happen. My reliance on the walking stick began to decline. Steadily I began to walk on my own without it. In September I sent the "toko" (walking stick) home to Fiji in a parcel carried by a friend who was heading back. The first step in the Balsam Trees was in place. The next was seeing the sores heal up, and my leg for the first time since 1996 was healed!

Chapter 14

Judging and understanding; new friends in Sydney

As for the characters I met in Sydney, first there was the Palestinian, and a relationship which grew was with the local Lebanese and Arab as well as refugee communities in Sydney. I went through a dilemma of why I have Muslim and refugee friends from all over and nothing happened to me. In fact, the time from 2000-2004 the refugees and migrants were actually the majority of my Australian-based friends and there have been no incidents between us which brings me to a few conclusions. The disgusting and reprehensible behaviour by a few Lebanese guys in Sydney at the time I was there (the perpetrators paying for this from their own community, especially in jail) was the work of a tiny minority. Just like any other group in Australia, they had their idiots and sociopaths. In fact, I found a lot of the Lebanese and others to be much harder workers and more law-abiding citizens than most other Australians and a lot more patriotic for Australia. When I was in Darwin, out of 23 refugees I knew of, only 5 were on social security.

I don't take too much notice of the anti-Islamic paranoia gripping this country. There are several reasons for that. The first is that when I was at school we were absolutely afraid of nuclear war and those big bad Russian commies (we were frightened of the Russians in 1905 when the Tsar was in power, so much so that we built guns up on Thursday Island. And, the Russian Navy got slaughtered by the Japanese at almost exactly the same time!) Now we have the Muslims as our enemy and they are going to get their burkhas and take over, take the women and pillage the village!

I reckon those who take the bourka as an issue prove that they are devoid of any real issues to canvas. Why? Well, here's the jackpot; whilst the Christians are looking at that red herring, they ignore the real issues. In QLD, there was a departmental rule that kids couldn't talk about Jesus in schools. Though since rescinded it was amazing that in a Bible Belt State this could even get to the policy-makers without outcry!

I think that a lot of "Christians" back questionable politicians in a crusade against a non-existent threat! Even to the stage of demanding amendments to a section of the Australian Constitution, namely s116; that is the only guarantee of freedom of religion and from religion that if amended will make it open season on all religions not just Islam.

Sydney really solidified my stand to reach out to the Muslims and make friends with them as I did in Fiji. After 9/11 I made a special effort not to join the angry but ill-educated and mislead churchgoers who were going on the anti-Muslim crusade, and vowed to treat them with respect even if me and Islam just don't get on at all. You earn the right to share Christ. Walking around with an angry, ignorant attitude often fanned by images on Facebook, most of which are photoshopped doesn't cut it, my friends!

As I look at the law and the facts, it is becoming increasingly apparent that some politicians in Australia do not know even remotely what they are talking about when it comes to Islam, migration and refugees. The contrast here is between a first time writer and political commentator and student reading information freely available to anyone with a computer and politicians with the full weight of parliamentary information at their fingertips. The latter are deliberately playing very nasty politics as they choose to not do a basic research effort. It's a sad indictment on this country when leaders can't be honest and simply pick up their own laws and read them.

My argument is this, that whilst the politicians fanned the so-called Islamic threat, they ignored the enabler of it. The secular humanist government policies have taken Australia to a tipping point that is, for the first time, The majority of Australians voted recently voted for something which had only a few years prior been only discussed on the " Fringe " of Australian politics. This a clear indicator of how far the Australian nation has departed from its modern historical roots. This absence of any religion or religious consideration as to policy will naturally form a vacuum. Who will fill it is the question. I personally believe that Islam which, starting with the traders from Indonesia who traded with the Aboriginals of the Top End, which has long history of interaction with Indigenous Australia but has never managed to settle or penetrate Australias pre settlement culture. This is in spite of having, at one time, the largest non-Aboriginal population in SA, NT, and Western Qld! I believe that to stop the hypothetical threat turning into a reality one must first start to ensure that there is an acknowledgement that modern Australia is founded on Christian Principles. Populist Politicians should read what they are talking about before seeking amendments to sections of the constitution that affect everyone to catch a non-existent threat!

Another group I began to see more of were the homosexual

community and I have actually ended up with several of them as friends. My relationship with them is heavily influenced by how a few of my church friends have sons and daughters who are homosexual. Their way of dealing with what is a huge discrepancy in lifestyle has inspired me. I know what the Bible says about the homosexual lifestyle and can't really shy from it. However, the fact is that a lot of well-meaning Christians don't do the church a favour to them either. They present ostracism rather than love, and tolerance instead of genuine friendship that earns you the right to talk to them in a meaningful way. Why use the word tolerance? That's because tolerance means grudging acceptance of something rather than acceptance. In the way this word is mistranslated today, the seeds are sown and the indirect truth is told of what's really there.

Isn't it time friendship and love replaced tolerance? Then, and only then, will the church be able to lovingly talk about the issues of homosexuality. Until then it will be opposed and shut out. That is a long way away from where I stood on this matter before becoming a Christian. In the 1980s I used to say a firing squad was the only solution! Also, Jesus was faced with the same attitude as I had from people who one would have thought knew better. When the scribes who were Pharisees saw Jesus eating with people, everybody tolerated at best and ostracised them at worst. They asked His disciples, "Why does He eat with tax collectors and sinners?" Hearing this, Jesus told them, "It is not the healthy who need a doctor, but the sick. I have not come to call the righteous but the sinners" (Mark 2:16-17).

Therefore, where should a man who professes himself as a Christian sit? Where Jesus sat, of course. There are a lot of churches and "Christian groups" that Jesus would not attend.

Chapter 15

When they build the Railway

The Alice to Darwin Railway was something of a joke in the Territory. It was promised but never seemed to be built. Therefore if something was out of reach but needed to be done, I would say, 'I will get that done when they build the Alice to Darwin Railway', which meant either never or don't hold your breath for it. I planned to do one last trip to Darwin before attempting to return to Fiji in June 2001. I left Sydney with no walking stick and no sore on my leg and went to Melbourne to see my mother and brother's family. My cash ran out and I put my credit card through to get my ticket to Wilcannia. It approved! At Wilcannia I purchased another ticket to Alice Springs, again no cash, but approved! My stay in Broken Hill New Year's night 2001, approved. Remember, no cash in the card!

Whilst en route to the Territory, something arose that slammed the brakes on me returning to Fiji and I began to think whether or not it would be smarter to use the time in Australia to resume my university studies if possible, either in Sydney or in Darwin. At Kulgera I called Watiqu's brother and told him it was unlikely I was going to keep to schedule and return by June. In Alice Springs I stayed with a friend of mine and did a bit of work with Geoff Miers. I went out to Hermannsburg and paid my respects to Kummanjayi and then returned to Alice Springs.

There was another reason why I did that trip and stayed a week in Alice Springs. Remember "The Gospel in accordance to Ranadi"? Well, as I said, it was believed by maybe a quarter of Watiqu's family and others that she shared it with. My trip was to clearly demonstrate that if it was true, "payback" would have effectively made Alice Springs and Hermannsburg a no-go zone. In fact, the whole NT would have been out of bounds because I would have possibly been killed one way or another! To prove the point, I took a photo of myself at Hermannsburg and mailed it to the pastor at Watiqu's church. Then on January the 20th I boarded the bus to Darwin.

It was at Ti Tree, 190km North of Alice Springs, that I'd made the decision to remain in the NT and effectively reset everything; the whole situation in Fiji had become untenable. At Tennant Creek I informed the mob in Ba that I was not coming back to Fiji and was planning to resume my degree, so when circumstances permitted I could return to my family and Watiqu. I decided to give it three years before either we divorced or I was back with Watiqu in Fiji.

When I came to Darwin I was met by an old friend, and a place at the Salvation Army in Mitchell Street was there for me. I called the hostel my miracle stops because in a town where there were waiting lists galore I always got a place there. I then restarted at the university and moved into the student quarters at NTU; a miracle because they let me pay off my bond! That just never happens.

Here I recommenced university to complete the "missing link" of eleven units that I was forced to abandon in 1996. Firstly, there was a few tidy up jobs to do which meant I had to repeat four of the units I did prior to 1996 in order to boost my marks up. Secondly I was under pressure from the deteriorating situation in Fiji with my marriage, and thirdly there was only prayer to get me through the university studies. My first semester was one unit then the next was two. My head injuries from my accident in 1996 made it impossible to do any more so progress was going to be quite slow.

Meanwhile, things between me and Watiqu deteriorated and though I was to keep the maintenance flowing for another year I had to shift gears a lot to do it. For a start, the builder who ripped us off with the house in Ba also ripped off his suppliers who then chased me. This pushed my financial situation over the edge. I was forced to default on my debts in Fiji including the house. The bank there did something unprecedented. They gave me a year's grace to get our act in order financially.

At this time, I was committed to keeping my marriage alive and genuinely thought that if Watiqu decided to use the tools and other bits including the house itself to produce an income, we could trade out of trouble financially and make the 400 a month mortgage commitment when it fell due in a year's time. However, this was not to be. Watiqu seemed far more interested in relying on the money from Darwin (though I told her it was not reliable repeatedly) and though my marks and everything else were improving, the situation with my marriage was not. Still 28 per cent of my money was going to Fiji in one form or another and how I managed to feed, clothe myself, and pay my rent was a miracle in its own right.

In July I ended up with a bicycle! A 26-inch mountain bike which I started riding around Darwin. I got a new bike, a ladies step-through because my leg had problems going over a top bar. In October I built a trailer for it and it became a common sight around Darwin. "Funny bike" was what the kids called it at my church, the COC in Berrimah on the outskirts of Darwin. It served as a trolley ride for the Indigenous kids anywhere I went. To get there involved a 13km ride one way twice a day, so return was 26km. There was also a bit of work there too and the pastor was quite gifted in terms of entrepreneurship and teaching so I thought I'd ended up in the right place and stayed there for two years. As far as church was concerned, I'd attended the old church twice when I returned to Darwin; the last time was to see Pastor Dennis voted out. To me there were too many good memories and it hurt me to see it like it was then. I attended Faith Centre as well so was unsettled for a while for the first six months I was back in Darwin. The rest of 2001 went OK and we had peacekeeping troops from East Timor stationed in Darwin from Fiji.

Most of them were good blokes with often hard pasts and families far away. They had served in places like Lebanon and were often the only UN force respected by all sides. Fiji's part in the world is like that. A small isolated country that's respected for its evangelism and peace making abilities. I will always maintain that the first seeds of the Middle East Peace Treaty was started on a nondescript table in Qana in the place Jesus turned the water into wine, with the Israelis, Hezbollah and others who met therewith the Fijians. They were the only peacekeepers who got on well with all parties in the conflict.

I keep an eye on current affairs, I have since childhood. This placed my general knowledge way ahead of where the odds said it should be. Of particular interest to me was the Soviet involvement in Afghanistan and of course regional politics in the Asia and Pacific. It was interesting to see who backed who in these wars in Afghanistan and Iraq. Then after the Soviets left, the news media moved on to other things. When the Iran/Iraq war was on I noticed with interest that the US backed Saddam Hussein, even reflagging his oil tankers to prevent Iran from attacking them.

Over the next decade there was a slow burning fuse in both Iraq and Afghanistan in particular as groups took advantage of what was a civil war zone that was awash with guns and anarchy and a people yearning for peace; any peace. No one, it seemed, really cared about the situation when the Cold War was over and the Soviet Union had gone to the trashcan of history and that was seemingly that.

The night of the 11th of September 2001 was an unusually muggy night, even for Darwin. I was at the student quarters when the news came through, and I initially thought that a Cessna or small transport had hit the World Trade Centre. A look at the computer an hour later showed me that it was a lot more serious than I thought it was.

Suddenly there was outrage, but not directed against those who deserved it, namely the terrorists, as well as those who must have been grossly incompetent that let them get away enough to let them get away with the biggest attack on the US since Pearl Harbour in terms of loss of life. Whether they did that deliberately or not is the stuff of many conspiracy theories and thus is outside the realm of this book. There was an explosion of indignation against Muslims in general. However, Darwin being Darwin, we did not see the backlash as it's a very multicultural place and everyone fitted in well.

My views on it and the circumstances that surrounded it were shaped by the facts I'd mentioned earlier. A group called Midnight Oil wrote a song called "Short Memories". Yes, everybody forgot about what happened a decade earlier. Often I was called a traitor because I was not accepting all of

President Bush's reasons. As it turned out in the case of Iraq, I was right and right again in the case of Afghanistan. What people don't understand is when you dump your "Allies" they end up gravitating to the next group that offers order and legitimacy.

In both Afghanistan and Iraq, groups backed by the West formed the Taliban which was set up by the US backed ISI in Pakistan. ISIL was almost the same. A vacuum was filled by that group. Such is historical fact. Whether it's Bougainville, the Bali Bombings, ISIS, or the Taliban, the reason these wars kept going is far more detailed than what the mass media will tell you. I was and am opposed to Australias involvement in Afghanistan and Iraq and other wars geographically far from Australia that produce no end result except make the enemy one is fighting stronger whils wasting a hell of a lot of money and lives. Like Vietnam, I respect the brave men and women who have sacrificed often with their lives in these wars. They are heroes who, like Aussies throughout the 20th Century and this one, have punched well above their weight and had the respect of friend and foe alike. However, those who send them there should think of the expense and the hardship these brave soldiers are being sent to and for what reason. However, my views were not welcome in most company.

At the end of 2001 I met an Indonesian lecturer and his wife and they let me house-sit for three months. I love dogs and they had a Labrador which I gave the run of the place not knowing precisely the rules for him in the house. I also found out I could drive a car! I backed Richards's car out of the driveway and found I could operate the controls. After they came back I moved out of the student quarters into a place in Nightcliff, but the landlord was always sticking her nose through the door every couple of days. This was a clear breach of the Tenancies Act in the NT but I decided not to rock the boat as she was Fijian and had influential connections there. I therefore relocated to another place which was better.

On the 1st of January 2002 the money going to Watiqu was cut off when my finances finally toppled over. It was not to resume for another six years. The bank took the house in Fiji as well but again was generous in letting everybody stay put until the house was sold. Every attempt to bring things into a workable solution in our marriage woes failed and in 2002 I filed for divorce with the family court in Darwin.

I had about two years between my divorce and remarrying in total from when I left Fiji in 2000 to 2004. The likelihood was that it was going to be quite some time before I saw anyone in Fiji again, and the fact that my finances could by now only look after number one, every time I did an essay I needed to pray a lot to do them. The grades kept rising, with only one pass represented in the units I had completed since resuming university in 2001, the rest were credits, distinctions and high distinctions.

Getting a driver's licence for a car was my very own version of the pie in the sky; the finances were not there to get one but there were jobs available for me if I did get a driver's licence in the 80s and 90s. I asked the then CES whether or not they could assist in getting the finances together as part of a work agreement. After all there was a driver education programme in the NT. The answer was no. I told them the fastest way to get me into work was to enable me to get a driver's licence. Any fool could see that, I thought. Well, I thought wrong.

Remember the title of this chapter? My joke ran that I would get my licence when the Alice Springs to Darwin

Railway was built as I regarded both as distinct impossibilities. Well, God has a firm sense of humour. The licence, the car and the Alice to Darwin Railway all came along at around the same time. However, on the day I took delivery of the car and got my licence, my divorce with Watiqu came through: 15th of May 2002. When I went back to Fiji in 2015 Watiqu said we were still married and the divorce had no effect in Fiji. The fact is that the Fiji Family Law Act says the divorce is valid. I hope Watiqu can get on with her life.

The car of my prayers was a four-cylinder Toyota Camry bought with a loan. At first I drove it between Darwin and Katherine on a pay day. However, my real goal was the fact that in my time I had managed to get three quarters of the way around Australia between us arriving in 1969 and 2002. The only gap left was between Katherine in the NT, Kununurra, Broome, Port Hedland, and North West Cape and Exmouth in WA. That's a distance of about 3,000km of road in the second biggest state on earth (you could fit Texas, Alaska and Colorado in this one and still have plenty of room left). At the end of 2002 I drove from Darwin to Port Hedland and then on to Exmouth stopping at our old house in Exmouth opposite the hospital there. I was now the first Gregory to have gone around Australia on the tarseal and possibly the first in our family to have a university degree!

I went to Perth then across Australia to my mum's in Victoria where I found work with an old Alice mate of mine before heading north through Port Augusta to Alice then on to Darwin. An 8,900km round trip. My car got a name; Adi Lewa, Chiefly Woman; a name that's stayed with my vehicles and the colour, blue over green over white. Melanesian colours. In 2003 I finished my Arts Degree; before the accident I was getting credit and pass scores. Post-2001, when I resumed the degree, my score was a credit average. After I left Darwin, I went to WA and returned to Darwin via Qld where I patched up some long overdue things and some former enemies became my friends at last. I should have done the trip sooner! My policy was, and still is, that deciding to forgive is often the only option. Forgiveness of others is a major deal when addressing a story like mine.

Chapter 16

Winning your impossible war; how to prevail.

Remember the section marked "Asking the Impossible: are you ready?" OK, here's where we get to the next half of that section, the battle itself. Picture if you may: you have managed to survive in an extremely hostile environment against high odds. Many of your friends are no longer with you and died younger than you and often violently. However, you believe in Jesus and put your trust in Him to get you moving in the right direction. You are not equipped to do the task you are planning to do and part way through it you have a huge accident where the first major miracle is that you are not a quadriplegic. Abandoning your studies, you go to your girlfriend and within two years you have two ex-wives, a child in Fiji and are back in Darwin broke!

How do you resume things from there?

Well, here are a few verses of the Bible you can build a strategy on:

Philippians 4:17 "I can do all things through Christ Jesus who strengthens me."

Psalm 28:7 "The LORD is my strength and my shield; my heart trusts in him, and he helps me. My heart leaps for joy, and with my song I praise him."

Proverbs 3:5 "Trust in the LORD with all your heart and lean not on your own understanding."

Matthew 17:20 "He replied, 'Because you have so little

faith. Truly I tell you, if you have faith as small as a mustard seed, you can say to this mountain, 'Move from here to there,' and it will move. Nothing will be impossible for you."

I have studied law and hold a law degree. As I mentioned earlier, in law when you present a case you have to use other cases before yours to back up your argument. These are where the judgement is in favour of your case but in other related cases. It's called the Law of Precedent; it applies more so as you engage the impossible task before you. Consider the following questions to set your precedent.

1. What has the Lord shown you about your life?

2. What has your history of His divine protection and guidance looked like?

Have you got a good memory of where the Lord's answered your prayers in difficult situations? To start this section there must be an attitude of gratitude. After all you have managed to survive and form a plan to work with. Planning involves teachability which is one thing that's definitely needed for this. Listening and learning from those wiser than yourself is a must. I've found that even those who don't like you have often had a very valid point that you must work on. If you want to end up failing and possibly dying, don't let anybody tell you anything or show you anything.

Here's a few points:

1. An answer to prayer is a blessing and is direction, not necessarily approval. Even His *no* is a blessing.

2. *No* is still a word from God in season. I had fourteen occasions when I felt divine direction in my life and three of those were a rebuke, four of them were a *no*, and believe me several months on I was praising Him because the path I asked for would have destroyed me. It's critical to listen to the Lord and whoever He sends. I didn't, and the consequences were not good.

3. Listen to other people and make yourself accountable to others as well as God.

4. Take authority over any rebelliousness, pride and other inhibitions that will prevent or sabotage your walk with Him.

5. Have an *Attitude of Gratitude;* this is utterly critical for your very survival. An attitude problem will make you stop praying and the devil to start preying on you!

Bible verses such as the ones below are definitely worth remembering:

Psalms 107:1 "Give thanks to the LORD, for he is good; his love endures forever."

Deuteronomy 12:7 "In the presence of the LORD your God, you and your families shall eat and shall rejoice in everything you have put your hand to, because the LORD your God has blessed you."

Philippians 4:4 "Rejoice in the Lord always and again I say rejoice."

Psalm 23:5 "You prepare a table before me in the presence of my enemies. You anoint my head with oil; my cup overflows."

Colossians 2:15 "And having disarmed the powers and authorities, he made a public spectacle of them, triumphing over them by the cross."

Philippians 1:6 "Being confident of this, that he who began a good work in you will carry it on to completion until the day of Christ Jesus."

These Bible verses have been very important to me.

Of course, afterwards a thought occurs to you: "You've survived against impossible odds and batted way above your weight! The atheists and knockers around you cannot explain your survival because to admit the miracle would be an acknowledgement that not only God exists but Jesus does too! Those who have helped you, and there are so many, are always mentioning you because they too are amazed!"

If it wasn't for Jesus, I'd be in a coffin box years ago! Or a vegetable!

Give thanks for even the small things. A song written by an Australian man *"From little things big things grow"* is not a Christian song but it's inspired me to be grateful for small beginnings!

Chapter 17

Elliott: A town that cries out

In this chapter I have altered names of people. Otherwise the chapter is entirely factual.

I was aiming to get back to Perth but was stopped at Mt Isa after going through the Gulf country in QLD. I ended up driving 650km with a gearbox full of water after I went through a flood near Camooweal. I was in Tennant Creek when the first train rolled through town and I got a telling off by the caravan park owner because I was all over the TV! A relationship was starting with a lady from Elliott resulted in the caravan park owner throwing me off the place with the lady being Aboriginal being the main reason.

Radini came into my life with a little boy. My history of romance was not a good one but I felt at last could get on with my life. Fiji had collapsed totally and there was no way I was going back there anytime soon; no money and very, very hurt. Radini and I met and after a very brief courtship opposed by a lot of her white friends in Tennant Creek as well as in Elliott we got married on the 6th of May 2004.

Radini and I moved first to a flat in Tennant, then to her sister's house in Elliott. There was opposition to us in Elliott and the local pastor in training who was a local Aboriginal leader, now deceased, told me a few things about a conversation he had with a friend of mine. I rang the friend up and caused a rumpus from Marla to Tennant to Darwin as he told both the bloke in Elliott and the bloke in Tennant not to drag his name into things. Adi, Radini's sister, was invited to Marla as an act of goodwill to us from the pastor there.

Well, it's said you can only give what you have. If I have dirt, I can't give gold. The AIM church at the opposite end of town down the road had a better following than the AOG and they were anti-Pentecostal. In fact, the Tennant Creek church had people in it I either used to drink with in Alice or who had a strong impact in my life at that time (in the 80s). The person in the latter case had fallen away from Christ. The church had great musicians but used to play CDs of praise and worship. I wondered what was going on. It was weird. They also had no place for traditional instruments. I reckon that in heaven the didgeridoo and clapping sticks will be there being used and God Himself will enjoy the sound!

Elliott, a small town in the middle of the NT, formed a supply base during World War Two. Almost on the match line, that is where desert vegetation meets the savannah of the "Top End". It has quite lovely scenery around it with the NT's largest lake just 20km away and the Newcastle Waters Station just 26km north. It has a lot of history and was the crossing point of Aboriginal trading tracks of old that later became the stock routes from WA to QLD and from north to south.

A soak named Wallamanda has deep significance to many Aboriginal groups hundreds of kilometres distant. Imagine that Vanua Levu in Fiji is about 4,000sqkm in area, well Newcastle Waters station was as big as that. With its sister stations it was actually larger than Fiji or Israel with 50,000 cattle and about 150 people on all three stations. I loved the place and I love the scenery. There was also a migratory bird route with magpie geese and pelicans; the pelican being the de facto symbol of the town.

Elliott had three distinct areas; Gurungu North, Gurungu South and the white area in between. The town had two large organisations; a government of Self Preservation called Gurungu Council whose CEO disliked me from the start as I saw what he was up to. There was also the Elliott District Community Council dominated by the white people who, other than the Ampol, held a strangle hold on the place. The race relations were such that the "Gaza border" as I called the strip of land between Gurungu North and the town could have been a walled border because the whites didn't know much about the Indigenous community and vice versa; it was 300 metres wide but might as well have been a few miles!

Speaking of churches, there was the Aboriginal Inland Mission, run by a local Aboriginal bloke named Harold Daly Waters who was the local police officer. There was a branch of the church in Tennant Creek mentioned earlier run from Tennant Creek under a pastor in training who was put in the job even though he was not able to carry it out. To put new converts into positions of authority in the church is expressly forbidden by the Word (see 1 Timothy 3:6).

Of course, there was the huge Mormon presence there a few years prior. At one time 80 per cent of the community were Mormon. In fact, the Elliott library still had the outline of the old lettering on the wall as it was the HQ of the Mormons in Elliott. Just before we came on the scene, a couple who owned the town's only op shop were involved in child sexual abuse in the community and when he and his wife left they got Radini to take over the op shop they ran.

The Elliott community was in the national media for child abuse and neglect four times whilst I was there (ABC 4 Corners and the Bulletin were two occasions). There were 54 Foetal Alcohol kids born there whilst I was there. That's out of a population of 400! A community where there were 57 out of 85 dwellings structurally unsound from the start. A community where the leadership burned out from lack of support. Outsiders often either joined the community's circles and went along or burnt out fast.

Even non-Christians used to comment on the leaden atmosphere that hung over the place when they went through. The shops had a reputation I found out about when I was driving across the Nullarbor in 2003 and I stopped at Cocklebiddy Roadhouse in WA, a typical one house town in the middle of nowhere. 'Don't stop in Elliott, especially at this place', someone told me. The problem was that with a captive clientele of 390 people there was no real need to be reasonable and the reputation of the place was the topic of many a conversation on the UHF transceiver radio that formed the staple of a long distance driver in Australia. Simply, if you want to treat people badly the news gets around fast. I am glad to say that several businesses have changed hands and things have got better since I left.

I didn't know it but within seven years Radini and I would be burned out and separated. As for the pastor-in-training, well, several verses come to mind. The one that stands out most is, "God is not mocked; You will reap what you sow" (Galatians 6:7). The man kept on going off the rails with his life at a huge variance at what his calling was. A man who could have been a great leader was instead a hostile belligerent. In late December 2004 he started a riot in the community in which both Radini and myself were hit by him with a steel jack handle. With our relationship within the AOG being what it was, the situation warranted no surprise. However, he was soon forced to leave town.

The Pentecostal church effectively died after that. The

man was warned repeatedly by prophesy and one day in 2007 he collapsed over the steering wheel of his car at his uncle's place. He's not the first person who has been cavalier with the things of God who I've seen come to an identical end. As is the case of a lot of people, what offends me most was that the man had a lot of talents and could have been a fine leader. The thing that really upsets one in places like Elliott is the waste of good people. People who, if listened to and their great talents harnessed instead of being left to burn out and rot in the system I call Welfare Colonialist Genocide, could really change this great land for the better; for all of us.

We went to Katherine and the impact of the assault had my right eye out of focus and I couldn't drive so Radini drove. In Darwin the Lord healed my eye just as we were being tested for it! We spent Christmas up in Darwin then drove back to Elliott. The house that housed the pastor and his family was empty and the way the police conducted themselves warranted a complaint to the Ombudsman which, like the complaint to the tenancy tribunal and Consumer Affairs throughout the time I was in Elliott, lead nowhere. Of course, one can see what the Aboriginal people think of white man's law when a NT thing called the Berrimah Line precludes a satisfactory addressing of problems.

The Berrimah Line is a hypothetical line at the suburb of Berrimah behind which the NT Government cared about and south of it they didn't. These days I call it the Adelaide River Line, about 100km south of Darwin as Darwin has grown quite large since 1985. Too Black Too Remote seems to be the way Darwin's government deals with its communities regardless of who is elected. This neglect led to the Federal Government taking over functions of the NT in a controversial initiative called the Intervention in 2007.

Radini began to work for a commonwealth government department in Elliott but her health made her very unreliable. My own fight with diabetes and struggling to juggle everything as a result of it has taught me a lot. Slowly both this and burnout took their toll. Radini was a lady that had taught me heaps and loved me, but we were slipping apart as the pressures of the community and issues in the family took their toll. We tried a geographical solution and moved up to Marlinja which was a lot better in some ways but not others. I still love the place though the number of times I approached the Minister for Housing up in Darwin as well as Minister for local government about non-existent water, bad housing construction and other issues were legion.

Eventually after I left, they fixed the Marlinja water, or so I thought. 500,000 dollars it cost them. Guess what? My garden hose water pipe plumbing was still in use in 2015, three years after I left and featured on Fiji One TV! A lot of people in Rakiraki and elsewhere commented on it as they are not used to an Australia where nothing worked and everything fell apart and nothing was really done to remedy it.

My involvement with the affairs of Gurungu Council was to last five years. Gurungu Council was hard fought for. A battle by the community elders that lasted about three years. On the surface it was fair logic to argue against it. Two organisations offering similar overlapping services in a town of 400 people or so. However, that was just one side of the coin and in itself doesn't even begin to establish a true picture. The town had a reputation for being racist and exploitative. In fact, it had a nickname with Aboriginal People: "Little Alabama." Without Gurungu the place would be run by a group of ten white people completely. Many communities like Elliott are like a ship with a crew that is divided into factions with an elite no one likes but have to obey.

The coping mechanism in a place like that is what is known as contracts of mutual exploitation. What's a contract of mutual exploitation? Well, it's a situation where both parties dislike each other but need the services of the other. Therefore, they attempt to get along. Picture if you may a remote community where an Indigenous leader needs the access the white person can give and the white person needs the credibility and legitimacy that only the Indigenous leaders can furnish.

The story of Gurungu is one where apathy, lack of due diligence, and plain deliberate placement of unknowledgeable people can cause any organisation to collapse. The deliberate posting of ill-qualified people serves a purpose. It entrenches whoever is in an in-charge position as they then have to fix up mistakes and can often doctor reports from those below them. The CEO of Gurungu was a prime example of the fruit of those things. What shocked me was what he attempted to do to us and how he was hired. He put the hard word on me regarding the business that resulted in a complaint to the chairman of Gurungu. I then received a hand-delivered letter from his solicitor which I dismissed as troublesome but nothing else (a subject I had recently studied at Curtin was Media Law, especially defamation).

Things about him didn't stack up. For instance, for a man who purportedly worked for ELCOM in Lae PNG (which he told the council was a little village) not knowing any Tok Pisin was just the start. I found out he was hired on a phone call with no follow-up or reference checks. Radini, myself and other community members began to investigate, and then the CEO held a council meeting about how to get rid of me. The minutes fell into my hands after Radini took over as President and the CEO abruptly resigned leaving a huge financial mess and unpaid creditors and missing funds totalling up hundreds of thousands of dollars. For two days the fax bled unpaid invoices, up to the thickness of a phone directory. The administrators moved in as did a very decent bloke as CEO. He burnt out and was divorced by the time he left. When Gurungu was placed under administration, the accountant Gavin McCann did a great job in very stressful circumstances but still couldn't, even with the help of Gurungu's last CEO, turn the ship around. The organisation is now deregistered.

The community was full of the normal problems of small remote communities. However, people so used to being disregarded and trodden down, ripped off and bypassed, get apathetic and start a self-fulfilling prophesy where they have low self-esteem and the surrounding environment corrodes ability and leadership in what was one of the most talented towns I've ever lived in. Every community meeting I attended featured alcohol and the imposed restrictions on it as a major issue. Never mind the major issues that were there. There was a total lack of ability to engage in any initiative brought on by a welfare system that made good, talented, hard-working people into apathetic individuals who left town if they wanted to do anything. Either that or simply knuckle-under in a system where the profits often come at a price of your integrity and self-standing.

Chapter 18

How not to operate in another culture

A lot of non-Indigenous people who end up in places like Bougainville, Fiji, and Elliott in my view shouldn't have gone there in the first place. The reason why is amply demonstrated by my picture in a Fijian pocket of a Sulu that I used as my picture in the introduction of this book; it shows you how I expect expats to behave regardless of what country they are from. In the definition of an "Expatriate" I also include any non-Indigenous person on any remote community as they are not in the dominant culture anymore.

1. The people there can teach you a lot. I have a great appreciation for the things I was taught by the Mubarra people of Elliott, the Inkamalas, The Omeenyos, the Bowies, Watiqu's family, Ranadi's family, the people from West Papua, and many more. How to do things their way and learning the language and contributing rather than exploiting can make you a very appreciated person in the place rather than a point of resentment. Such ways can have a major effect on the place you are working in. It can even change a volatile situation where expatriates are a lightning rod or part of one. (A lightning rod is a point of focus of resentment, e.g. the war memorial in Elliott built when everything else was in such a poor condition. It

was seen as a waste of money by many and was vandalised as a result several times.)

2. Practise what you preach. On many cars in Australia I see, "Fit in or **** off" stickers. OK, if you are going to Bali, PNG, Fiji or other overseas place, even as a tourist, do what you would want the people to do in Australia. Learn the language, eat the food, make friends and be sensitive to the local culture. Either that or stay home. If you marry a Filipino for example, learn Tagalog. If you can't do that because you are too culturally proud to learn the other person's language and traditions, marry an Australian of your own ethnicity. Problem solved.

3. Don't think of yourself as the one with all the knowledge.

As for a situation where none or a few of the above were applied, there is no better example of this than what happened in the Pentecostal church in Elliott. The pastor-in-training mentioned before told the oversight in Tennant Creek a few lies. To handle the supposed insurrection, the pastor in Tennant Creek sent up some Grey Nomads, old people with a Gypsy-type lifestyle (I've done this myself and still do) sent up from NSW.

They committed a few cardinal sins of missionary work in remote areas. First, they took sides politically; second they asked too much of Gurungu, with which the pastor-in-training was a senior officer. Thirdly, they assumed that they would be teaching a group of White Australians. All deadly sins and fatal errors. There are many Aboriginal languages in Australia and all very different from Barkinji in

Wilcannia to Yolngu in Arnhem Land to Warlpiri in Central Australia. These people knew Jingulu/Mudburra as a first language, not English, and they had more spiritual awareness than the "great white missionary" sent up to "enforce things" as the man said to me. We did have a church in the teacher's house.

The "Travelling Show" as I called these old folks wrecked it within a week and when we simply didn't want to listen to their rubbish he turned up at our compound with the pastor from the parent church in Tennant Creek and a few others. He waved his hands in the air and acted like he was quite insane in front of not one, but three leader's houses in Elliott. He then proclaimed, 'I release you to the devil in the name of the Lord Jesus Christ.' Well, he released me to God because what I saw of the church there was not reflecting the Jesus I served, and even today I see his antic as an act of liberation from a church that simply couldn't abide by its own rules.

When I left Elliott I found that he had no authority to do what he did and he wasn't even a pastor. What he did do though, was leave a sour taste in everybody's mouths. When he returned the next year, Gurungu wouldn't give him the facilities and he pounded the table of the CEO. I was in the driveway of the office and Radini was at the housing officer's desk and I could hear him shouting quite clearly. Eventually, he got put behind the Ampol and didn't do much at all. 'Those Christian bludgers' was an average remark about them in town by Indigenous and non-Indigenous alike. However, Radini and I had our involvement in that church brought to a halt for many years afterwards, even long after we had separated.

There were many gifted people in the church in Elliott but they were unable to effectively utilise those gifts. The main reason was the "gate keeper" mentality of many at the church which would prohibit anything they thought was of the devil. Things such as musical instruments like the Didgeridoo. My view on this has been previously noted and once again I reiterate, I look forward to hearing the Didgeridoo and clapping sticks played in heaven. The tragedy is that the mindset of the "great white missionary" is still a staple of many ministries and more so in secular policies and interactions involving Indigenous people. These "great white missionaries" can't seem to figure out that what is facing them has deep spiritual roots. They also have a long history of Christian ministry in their own right and could easily teach the rest of us a few things.

However, to my dismay they are not allowed and their ideas are quenched by mainly outsiders with a dated perception of who has the most to offer. People like the "Travelling Show" who surfaced in Elliott are more the norm than the exception. The often good name of the vast majority of hardworking missionaries who worked with and often protected the Indigenous population from attacks by settlers and from other forms of predation that formed an often ignored part of Australian History is irreparably ruined by the antics of those like the couple that made up the "Travelling Show"[4]. Another bunch of know it all white fellas who think they can train the people but instead leave them hurt and cynical of any church group that turns up. As for the many Indigenous and non Indigenous people who have become very cynical, I feel for you and am one with you in many ways. Your hurt and cynicism is the reason I wrote this book. As one of those

---

4   I met them in Inglewood in Qld and on the way through they saw me and scurried off like rats. Why? Well I decided that what happened in Elliott stayed there. In fact, I was looking forward to catching up with them over a coffee!

people who trod that path I sympathise with them. That is one of the key reasons I've written this book.

After the "Travelling Show" graced us with their presence the first time around, Radini and her sister settled into running the second-hand business which my mother helped out with by sending stuff up for us. This was an incredible shift for her and one I deeply appreciated. I did little but Radini and her sisters did a great job without a cent of government money going into the business. However, there is often an unwritten rule in these places and that is that Indigenous people are consumers and not business owners.

At first the whites in the town thought the business was temporary. However, after they started doing well the pressure came. Eventually we came back from Katherine one night to find the gate padlocked and no one assisted us to enable us to resume living in the caravan. The shop closed and whoever we went to complain to said that it was not their jurisdiction. This included a tribunal which one of my later lecturers was head of at the time. God gave us the first of three opportunities to leave Elliott. We had a place in Katherine offered to us by the Housing Commission but an event in Elliott influenced our decision to remain there. A decision that would come back to haunt us.

When I was in Elliott, I was quite dismayed as to the way people were treated by the shops and by many others who were supposedly there to be of service to the people of the community. Initially our involvement with Gurungu and the attempt to save it was as a result of genuine concern.

However, as time grew on I started to do things from a different motive — resentment — and the need to put what was a set of major problems in their place, especially the human ones that were in the community. On the surface the right motive, right? The motives behind my actions and the reason why I returned to university I had looked at after I left Elliott, and Radini and I separated, and I was asking why it fell apart when God has us together.

I stood for president of the town council and got trounced by the incumbent. I think this was a major mistake of mine. However, I told the local community that if the incumbent took over again Gurungu would close. He did and within six months Gurungu offices were closed and remained so.

It came down to three painful revelations:

1. **We fight not against flesh and blood but against principalities and powers.** I was trying to sort out all the problems by political means and using my own wisdom.

2. **Not doing what we were meant to do.** We prayed for direction but did not accept direction. Doors opened in Katherine and other places and we chose to stay for a number of reasons. When we eventually did leave, our marriage was finished, Radini went to Alice Springs and I went to Fiji. Likewise, we did not accept advice as to where to send a young lady in our care. We were warned of the school we were sending her to regarding its lax supervision. The consequences were not nice.

3. **Wrong motive for action.** The reason why I went back to university to study law was to get in a better position to get justice for the community. However, the motive was increasingly more to put people in their

place than it was a genuine attempt at fixing things. When I left Elliott that was very obvious to me.

Yes, there were problems way beyond our control such as the church situation, the community situation, and the family situation in some cases. Yes, all of those contributed to our demise in Elliott. But you have to take responsibility for your part in the failure, the buck does stop with you.

Chapter 19

The 50-metre-long ravens

In the Old Testament there is an account of a prophet running away from the wrath of a queen where he hid in a cave. When the food ran out, the Lord fed him with ravens flying in food for him (1 Kings 17:1-7). Well, the story of my time in Elliott has a real twist on the ravens-feeding thing!

The businesses in Elliot, with the support of a police officer, attempted to blockade us in 2009 by banning us from the only fuel outlet in town. The way they behaved disgusted so many people that there was no shortage of help for us and, like Elijah, we were being fed by ravens. Our ravens were the 50-meter-long road trains that brought us supplies. Road trains are a semi-trailer with usually two or even three trailers hitched up behind them. They are the backbone of the Outback. In fact, we were provided for so well that we didn't need the town at all! However, the situation was wearing us out. We were driving towards Elliott one day and I said to Radini, who was hesitating about leaving Elliott, that we should leave now or it would be heart-wrenching when our time came. That word turned out to be prophetic. I had made a complaint to the Racial Discrimination Commission regarding the roadhouse, and even though the case put pressure on him in contributing to his family's departure the case was dragged out. It was undermined not only by an unwillingness of people to testify but also because I felt sorry for the bloke and his family.

To illustrate the reasons why these people ended up the way they did and my response towards their deeds was rather reluctant at best, I will use the examples below to illustrate the point of what happens when people don't do the right thing.

A bloke from Romania named Richard Wurmbrand had a similar opinion regarding Nicolae Ceausescu, the dictator who sent many Christians to be tortured and put in jail in his country, Wurmbrand included. The man who was to rise up and be the dictator that imprisoned Richard for thirteen years was badly mistreated by a Christian mob who should have known better. A look at the biographies of dictators like Dos Santos in Angola, Sonora Machel of Mozambique, Mugabe of Zimbabwe, Pol Pot of Cambodia, and Stalin all ring with this horrible truth of what happened to Ceausescu. To think that what happened in the Congo (Kinshasa) would never have happened if people like Patrice Lumumba were treated with respect by those who had a holy duty to do so.

The relevance of the above was that the owner took over the roadhouse from a South African family who had been managing it. He brought his family, including a young boy, and we got on well for about a year after he came along. However, my dump-scrounging unearthed some records he threw out that showed that his new purchase was in fact in trouble. "Book ups" or credit given to the local community had not been paid since the old managers left. The total was about 21,000 dollars.

The young boys in the community bullied the young boy which forced the owner to relocate him to Darwin. He who was seen as quite a reasonable man and very easy to work with when he came to Elliott was pushed into being a racist by the place's behaviour. That may distress some people but it's the truth and I can't shy away from it. I was very reluctant to take the action I did with the Racial Discrimination Commission because of this, waiting a year. Often people are pushed in the wrong direction by those who should know a lot better.

Yes, I wanted justice and wanted the community to see that white man's justice was not only words. However, as this dragged on, delay after delay, the reason for mounting the case was further undermined by us both leaving Elliott and my own marriage collapsing as it did. The case was withdrawn on the 17th of April 2012. Again I was left with a deep crisis of credibility in the law I was studying as it never seemed to work. When one hears news of a riot in a community, remember these lines before presuming you know why it happened or what you hear in the media.

Things had slidden in my own life to such an extent that I simply didn't like the way I was doing many things in the place. I was praying daily for an end to the constant apathy and the corrosive effect the general malaise had on all of us and our ways. One day it came, "Mene Mene Tekel Uparsin" (God has weighed, numbered your days and divided the kingdom) (Daniel 5:25). It's interesting that is what happened in Marlinja after I left.

The suppliers stopped supplying though I was in good standing with them for three years. I was worried that what happened to the roadhouse owner, and quite a few people who were actually sympathetic to the Aboriginal cause, was going to happen to me. They start well then burn out, becoming racist and bitter shells who time serve if they stay. Eventually they burnt out and became resentful, racist and bitter. Thanks to Jesus I never got to that point. The facts remained that a geographic change was warranted if Radini and I was going to survive as the great couple we were, and I have no doubt that if we had done that change, Radini would be writing this book with me rather than me writing it on my own in Perth.

There was a prediction made by a prophetic teacher just before everything caved in that there was going to be a major shift due to my wishing to see some changes in Elliott. At the time I thought we could play it out and resolve things reasonably well and besides, I'd withdrawn the ADC case. However, major issues closer to home needed addressing. Major ones that in my opinion, and to others, warranted the intervention of the authorities that were not addressed and I simply could not bear to look at that any longer. We had four changes of house in seven years; "The Wandering Jews of Elliott" was what I called us. In all cases, I had done considerable work only to leave it behind to be burnt or otherwise destroyed and neglected. The attempts to set up Warlamarnda fell over repeatedly. In short, a mess. Too many passengers and too few people pulling the cart.

On the 8th of October 2011, I psychologically came crashing down; it was only 48 hours after my last exam. If it had happened earlier I'd have failed the semester. A similar thing had actually happened in mid-semester of 2018 and left me struggling to pass. The university was watching my health as it seemed as if I was going to seriously derail at any moment. Student Services had me in counselling. I had a Christian lady counselling me, which was a blessing especially as I am very distrusting of counsellors by nature anyway. This was a welcome change and started to restore some trust.

The phone calls dropped to very few between us and, despite Radini being in Darwin for a long time in 2012, she or her family never came to see me at the university. Soon there was no contact with them at all. I hoped everything could

Chapter 19

still work there after I left. In fact, it had stopped completely as no one had either the ability, the time, or the inclination to do anything about the corporation I had helped set up or anything else.

Not seeing any reaction from Elliott, I decided not to return to it that Christmas. I did not want any people in Elliott to know where I was. I turned off from the Stuart Highway at Katherine north of the river and drove to WA telling everyone in Elliott that I was taking leave of absence for one year. Things had deteriorated to that extent between Radini and I. From then on, we were separated. I decided that if worst came to worst, all belongings south of 16-degree parallel became theirs and what was north of it became mine, which was everything on the Ute they bought for me (the same one I drive now) and whatever was in Darwin as of the date I'd crossed the border. At least if things had resolved in Elliott then we could get back together again as I wanted so much to do and make our departure soon after that. To ensure we were not going too far, I said Radini could nominate any town within an 800km radius of Elliott. This meant that Darwin, Alice, Mt Isa, and Halls Creek were all candidates and all were within an easy ten hour drive of Elliott. In the meantime, I decided that the best policy was to get on with my studies and attempt to set things up better and simply give them space.

After going to Western Australia, I returned to Darwin to finish my law degree. Everything was very difficult especially as, since I'd left Elliott, the key reason for me doing it was gone. I began to seriously think as to why I was doing what I was doing and paying a high price. The Holy Spirit exposed the motive. I was going to use my newfound skills in a battle against the whites in Elliott and elsewhere. What was I there for? What was removed was an old motive and a new one replaced this.

I decided that rather than me going down there, to see if the old adage was true: that if someone loves you, let him or her go and see if they return. For some reason they did not even call me. Therefore, I had decided to withdraw from Elliott. An attempt was made to keep things going and I hoped that the progress made by the gang down there would hold with me gone. When I was there, I'd made a serious effort to teach them as they had lovingly taught me. I decided that my own choice was to stand down, withdraw from Elliott, and hope for the best. My official withdrawal date from Elliott was the 17th of April 2012, which was accomplished on time (though I had actually left in July 2011 not knowing that it would be permanent).

To this day, I find this subject hard to write about as it still hurts to think about it. It took years for me to emotionally recover from the separation. However, the breakdown before I went to WA was a narrow escape and I definitely didn't want to go through another one and the way things were going in Elliott there would have been a cast iron guarantee that I'd soon be knocked down for the count. On the 27th of June 2012, I decided to end my involvement with Elliott. When I returned from Qld for the new semester, Radini and I met up again. It was our last meeting. We formally divorced in 2014, not knowing who filed what and the papers missed each other. I burned mine when it was over in tears.

As for what was being done in Elliott, it seemed to simply stop. When I went through in 2014 to our old house in Marlinja, I saw everything abandoned, untouched and in place. I decided not to take any of it, as I was still very upset over the breakup of a good marriage. Radini has since remarried and

I definitely hope we can still be good friends. My response to Elliott was that I would respect whatever Radini chose to do and, if invited to reengage by her family with the community, I would work in and respect whatever she did regarding getting remarried. I had decided that in 2013 and unlike last time, I would stick to the task given.

I was on my breaks at university touring around with my Hilux and trailer. When I was in Qld in 2012, my old trailer had started falling apart. It had carried everything for a long time everywhere. I then got another one, an old abandoned project that I bought for $500. It has not let me down and I have gone around Australia twice with it.

In 2014 I had enough money to buy a new vehicle but the old Hilux was a gift from God that never lets up. An old 4-cylinder non-turbo diesel single cab is my last item other than memories, both good and bad, from Elliott.

In 2013 I returned to Fiji after a fifteen year absence. After a week with Watiqu and the three kids, I had to go up to Rakiraki and stay with my friends up there.

When I returned to Australia I did a zigzag trip, first to Townsville, then diagonally across to Adelaide then up to Darwin where I stayed at my former lecturer's property and at last, graduated with a Law Degree from CDU. My graduation, with the divorce from Radini going through at the same time, was not as great an occasion as I had liked. This was mainly due to the extended family no longer being with me. As I said earlier, it took about four years to properly recover and Radini and I have resumed communicating, though she is now remarried. I firmly believe in attempting to turn bad things into good things. In this case, that she, her new husband, the family, and I can be very firm friends, forgetting the past but looking forward to a better future. I should use this book in the spirit it's written to ask her forgiveness for my part in our break up that hurt us both so much.

I resumed living in Fiji in 2015, and sadly, the situation I had in 2013 and 1999 reasserted itself and I lost a lot of money in Fiji. Though I started meeting with a good crowd, this came too late to change the end of the game. I met Suliana in Fiji, who with her family has been no end of encouragement. Cyclone Winston Category 5 hit our village on the 22nd of February 2016 causing extensive damage but thankfully only one fatality that I know of in Rakiraki. My article on the 22nd of February 2016 regarding the cyclone was from what I know to be the first article published in the major print media from Rakiraki with the cyclone hitting only 12 hours before it was sent.

The way people helped each other and did heavy clean-up work, which in Australia would involve heavy equipment rather than manpower, has lifted my respect for those who were in it. An estimated 54 million Fiji dollars was raised domestically as well as assistance from Australia, New Zealand (which flew the first chopper over us a few days after the cyclone), and China. The dedication of the RFMF and the job they did in trying circumstances cannot be overlooked in the least.

As for Kathleen, after a long struggle to get her out of Fiji including an expensive but unsuccessful attempt in 2016, now lives in Sydney and is going well. Like those who provided for us in Elliott, many people have risen to the occasion here too and assisted Kathleen and us in Fiji. There have been a few people who helped Kathleen after she arrived in Sydney and even long before. Unfortunately the problem with money has effectively prevented my bringing her sister Gloria over and I hope that can be sorted out one day. At the time of writing, the possibility of me permanently returning to Fiji is slim. However, recent events have demonstrated that things can change fast.

Elliott has vastly improved since I left with belated attention from the NT Government gaining traction and the businesses engaging much better with the community. Again, I look forward to reengaging with the community and hope the tag of "Little Alabama" is, and remains, long dead. I long to return to Elliott and other communities whose people are such an inspiring part of my life as well as being some of the most challenging.

In 2016 I returned to Cape York and renewed acquaintances with some school friends up there. Again, former enemies are now best of friends and I look forward to one day working with them as I see the Lord open doors long closed. Old doors have opened again in Bougainville, PNG, and with Indigenous friends and relatives. I do pray that I can work through the challenges and be able to as a team make a difference to the way things are done.

Conclusion

I had decided to make this book last until 2014 as the rest of things are still going on. The miracles of provision and protection and of reconciliation are still ongoing and the Road of Life continues with my Lord at the wheel. May this book bring you into fellowship with this Lord of Miracles I worship and serve.

www.ingramcontent.com/pod-product-compliance
Lightning Source LLC
Chambersburg PA
CBHW021106080526
44587CB00010B/410